HOW TO CREATE THE LIFE YOU DESIRE

Antonio Ochoa

CONTENTS

ACKNOWLEDGMENTS

I would like to personally thank the following people for their contribution to the creation of this book:

Cash Keahey (editing and proofreading)

Johanna Schmidt (editing and proofreading)

Amy Shelby (editing and proofreading)

Touqeer Shahid (cover design)

Hammad Khalid (book formatting)

For those of you reading this, may your life be filled with freedom, health, wealth, and happiness

INTRODUCTION

We are **limitless**

By knowing a few simple truths about human nature and the universe, and by applying them in our everyday lives, we could potentially be, do, or have anything our hearts desire.

Most sensible people are looking for the most efficient way to get the best results in the least amount of time with the least amount of effort. We do this naturally when it comes to accomplishing any task or doing any kind of work. Over time, we incrementally find better and faster ways to get the results we want. However, when it comes to creating what we desire in life, many people forget their true potential as humans and end up choosing to do things the way they have always been done. This may be inefficient and cause much more pain than what is necessary. Sometimes, we may deny our own desires. We may hang on to our desires and just wait and wish for something to happen, taking no action toward that desire. We may give up and lose faith after failing too many times. We may be overwhelmed with doubts, worries, and ridicule in an attempt to imagine something better. We may not even know what we desire or lack the confidence to ask the universe for it. If you do not know what you want in life and you do not ask for it, chances are you will not get it. If you do know what you want and you constantly ask for it, you will most definitely get it. We just need to make sure we are asking in the correct way. The main problem I have noticed just by going about living my everyday life is that humans, as a species, have not yet learned the most efficient way to focus our creative energies and manifest our own desires. We all have the ability to manifest our desires. Just like learning how to do anything, there are specific methods to mastering the efficiency of the creative process. It is much simpler than some of the complicated things people do to fulfill desires in today's modern world.

After personally realizing this ability in myself, I started researching. Learning more about the topic, I began to make some amazing shifts in my life almost instantly. My shy demeanor and anxiety almost completely vanished. My home life started to change for the better. My performance at work had a significant improvement to the point where I started receiving a ton of recognition and rewards. My relationships with my true friends and my family grew stronger than they've ever been. Everything in my life began to shift in a more positive direction. The best part about it all was that I could go about my day-to-day life and truly be happy and confident with myself. Not to mention, for the first time ever, I was starting to see my main goals and desires slowly get closer and closer each day, which is a very exciting way to live.

Dale Carnegie is a very wise author and had an amazing understanding of the potential of us as humans. In his best-selling book, How to Win Friends and Influence People, he writes, "Compared with what we ought to be, we are only half awake. We are making use of only a small part of our physical and mental resources. Stating the thing broadly, the human individual thus lives far within his limits. He possesses powers of various sorts which he habitually fails to use." Carnegie was born in the late 1800s and died in the early 1900s. Obviously this man was way ahead of his time. In today's world, there is still no good reason why people are not yet up to speed on learning about this human potential, especially now that many people have an infinite amount of information available instantly at their fingertips with the internet. We are absolutely incredible beings and we all have amazing creative potential inside us already.

If we look at the people around us today, we will notice that there are those who are living in poverty, pain, frustration, and misery. On the opposite end of the spectrum, there are those living rich, happy, fulfilling lives. Some of us may want to consider the question: What separates the rich and happy from the poor and miserable? Why do some people seem to manifest desires so much better than others? There are certain truths about the universe that govern all of existence and those who have been taught to live by the truth, believe and understand the truth, will flourish in life, and experience miracles beyond imagination. Individuals who are ignorant or uneducated, or simply choose not to believe in the truth, are condemned by all the forces of the universe and will continue to experience unnecessary suffering until the necessary mindset and lifestyle changes are made.

As humans, we all have the freedom to access an infinite pool of energy and knowledge. Yet it seems that not many people take advantage of this knowledge, mainly because we never properly learn about what it is or how to use it. We are all taught to do so many things in our lives and we spend so much time learning and studying multiple different topics, many of which we never use in our everyday lives. Most people are never formally taught crucial skills like how to manage our own thoughts and emotions, create a significant positive impact on the world, change our habits to benefit ourselves and others, discover and achieve our own personal goals and desires, or overcome personal obstacles in our lives. Knowledge like this is available to all of us, and when we can finally access it, change begins to happen immediately. The world's population is slowly awakening and learning to master these abilities, but there still seems to be a large number of people who have not learned these fundamental lessons in life. Learning about these natural abilities that we all have is the next logical step in our evolution as humans. The sooner we evolve, the quicker we can move forward and change as a collective species to benefit the entire world and the entire universe.

There is so much to learn in this life and so little time on this earth to learn or experience everything for ourselves. Rick Warren, who is an American pastor and author, mentions in his 2002 book, *The Purpose Driven Life,* "While it is wise to learn from experience, it is wiser to learn from the experience of others. There isn't enough time to learn everything in life by trial and error, we must learn from the life lessons of one another." With a piece of information like this, we should be able to start looking in the right direction when it comes to learning and mastering any skill. We can learn a lot about ourselves and the universe on our own, but we can learn even more if we study and learn from individuals who already have this wisdom. Once I started learning and studying successful people in all fields of life, I began to grow my own wisdom more quickly than ever before. Before I started studying great thinkers and other people who seemed to have life figured out, I got most of my advice and information from people I knew personally, like friends, family, and other loved ones. This was an extreme setback now that I reflect on it, and it definitely limited the amount of wisdom and knowledge I was ingesting, simply because I was not learning from the best sources. Even though our loved ones may genuinely want the best for us, they do not always offer the best advice.

Most of us already have a general knowledge of the universe and our natural abilities as humans; some might even call it common sense. As far as we know, the truth about humans and the universe has been around for thousands of years and it has been passed down and translated through religions, teachers, parents, loved ones, and various other means. Some call it spirituality, some call it nature, some call it science. I see it all as general information that we can use to our advantage if, and only if, we can bring ourselves to believe it is true. We have used these truths about the human mind and the universe to advance our civilization beyond what anyone could have imagined. Spaceships that can fly thousands of miles away from earth and bring us back data from other planets, airplanes that can fly around the world on a single tank of fuel, cars that drive themselves. Even with the technology and information we have today, the human race is barely beginning to really understand what it all means, what to do with all of it, and how it is all connected. Because of the fact that only a few truly understand the limitless human potential, only a few can really teach it. By learning and connecting a few pieces of wisdom, we get a map or a key to all the abundance that the universe has to offer. With that key, we can begin to create a better world, and a better life for ourselves, and help the people around us do the same if we desire. Following the methods in this book and understanding the human mind and the universe will allow us to increase our access to the infinite energy of the universe and bring ourselves closer to becoming a limitless being.

Wayne Dyer, an author and motivational speaker, has a great way of describing how limitless people work. In one of his speeches, he says:

> *"Successful people, or no limit people, or self-actualizing people, or inner-directed people or whatever labels that have been put on them... these kinds of people are people who always have enough. There are some people who can handle anything, not because their circumstances are different. You see, your circumstances have very little to do with your fulfillment in life. It's how you're approaching your circumstances, it's your attitude toward your circumstances that make all the difference in the world."*

Many people have a misconception that our circumstances determine our reality, but as Dyer says, it is really the way we think and our approach to our circumstances that determine our reality. Oftentimes I hear people say things like "I could never write a book" or "I would never be able to work out four times a week" or "I can't *[fill in the blank]*" and what I always reply to those people is "not with that attitude." Approaching our circumstances with an "I can't" attitude will get us nowhere and keep us trapped exactly where we are. I still often catch myself with that same attitude, and each time I do, I am one step closer to becoming the best version of myself. If we can change the way we think and change the way we approach our circumstances, we can change our lives entirely.

Becoming a limitless person and living a limitless life is possible for anyone. To become limitless, there absolutely must be a true understanding of the relationship between oneself and the universe. Being a limitless person does not mean being absolutely perfect in every way. Perfection is an idea that all positive aspects will take over and replace all negative aspects. However, in reality, negativity cannot exist without positivity, and vice versa. Perfection is something that may be strived for but never achieved. There is always room for improvement and things can always be better, but perfection is not the ideal goal. Perfection is only an illusion or an idea in our mind. Trying to achieve perfection is like chasing a rainbow and hoping to find the pot of gold at the end of it; the rainbow just keeps getting farther away no matter how fast we appear to be approaching it. If there was a person who believed they were perfect, they would have stopped growing or changing, meaning they had cut themselves off from learning and becoming the next best version of themselves. True perfection is realizing that we already have and are everything we need to be successful and happy in life. True perfection is full acceptance of what is, unconditional appreciation for ourselves and the way things are now, and full willingness to change when change is appropriate.

It is also worth remembering that there will always be something that we don't know. Even if we have studied a single subject for thousands of years and can explain it very well, we still do not fully understand that subject. There is always more to learn, and there are always things that will be unexplainable and miraculous. That is the beauty of life.

The purpose of this book is not to convince anyone of anything. I am not a preacher and I do not wish to recruit you to any cult or religion. I am here simply to share a point of view that I find to be very valuable and worthwhile, in hopes that you can also see it as such. Everything that is about to be mentioned in this book is self-evident and shouldn't need any facts to back it up. With that being said, there are still going to be facts to support what you are about to read. Understand that you most likely will not agree with everything being said. The idea is to stay open minded and attempt to gain a better understanding of yourself and the universe by reading this book. While reading, it is not enough to simply read the words and accept them as truth, even though it may all seem very convincing. Study yourself and the universe around you in collaboration with this book to receive the most value. This book is designed to be simple to understand so that anyone can read it and learn the lessons without much effort. If there is any desire to know more about the source of these teachings, definitely check out Alan Watts and the other sources mentioned throughout the book.

> *"We hold these truths to be self-evident that all men are created equal."*
> *- The Declaration of Independence*

The beautiful part about all of this information is that anyone who truly wants to could start applying it today, right here and right now. Anyone can learn to understand these teachings, in any place of the world, with any background, religion, skin color, shape, or size. We all start somewhere different in life and all have a different story, limiting factors, beliefs, excuses, and obstacles in our environment. Regardless of the setbacks or limitations, we all have the same infinite potential to create great things in our lives. We all have something unique that nobody else has, and that is our own individual personality and perspective. No two people are exactly the same. Even if it doesn't seem like it, we are all exactly where we need to be for our own personal growth and development, and we are in the perfect place to move forward. Everything we need to unlock our full potential is right at our fingertips, only if we dare to reach for it and trust that there is a light at the end of the dark tunnel.

One lesson that I struggled with learning is that good things take time. We won't always see results right away when attempting to create change in our lives, and we don't get to eat the fruit the same day we plant the seed. If we really want to create the life of our dreams, we must have faith and trust that it will come in time.

Everyone is at their own stage of evolution and awakening, and there is no way to force somebody to evolve or awaken to the truth. You cannot help someone who does not want help and you cannot teach someone who does not want to learn. Awakening happens naturally and will happen at the perfect moment for each of us. The lessons and information in this book may challenge your current beliefs, but we can be sure that the intended message is only revealed to those who are ready to receive it. Reading this book is a sign to the universe that you may be ready for the truth.

Every day, new scientific discoveries are being made to reveal what we know to be true about humans and the universe. If your skepticism holds you back, you may still be able to discover your true potential by understanding these modern experiments. Joe Dispenza is one great modern-day source I have found. He produces real research with psychology and neuroscience to show how limitless and powerful humans really can be. He has found many ways to show scientifically how our brain and body are affected by our thoughts. Joe has helped people change their lives in ways that some might call miracles: helping cripple people walk, deaf people hear, and blind people see. I highly recommend researching him if there is any desire to dive more into the scientific evidence of human nature and how we work with the universe to create reality.

Dr. Daniel Amen is another inspiring modern-day example, who has completed very powerful research showing how our brain works and how it can change our life. Amen gave a Ted Talk, during which he said:

"So after 22 years and 83,000 brain scans, the single most important lesson my

colleagues and I have learned is that you can literally change people's brains. And when you do, you change their life. You are not stuck with the brain you have, you can make it better and we can prove it."

He continued:

"My colleagues and I performed the first and largest study on active and retired NFL players showing high levels of brain damage... What really got us excited was the second part of this study where we put players on a brain smart program and demonstrated that 80% of them could improve in the areas of blood flow, memory, and mood."

Dr. Amen's research also showed that people with very serious issues such as strokes, Alzheimer's, traumatic brain injury, addictions, obsessive-compulsive disorder, attention deficit hyperactivity disorder, anxiety, and depression can all overcome their problems in life just by changing the brain. By changing the way we think, and changing the way we look at ourselves and the world around us, we can completely transform and shift our lives for the better.

With proper guidance, we can take our mind and use it to create positive change.

There are many important lessons to be learned throughout this book and I believe that before anyone is able to fully take in the information and learn the lessons here, one must first understand detachment. One way to look at detachment is to imagine a man who falls off a high cliff along with a large rock. The man hopelessly and anxiously tries to grab onto and cling to the rock, hoping that the rock will somehow benefit him in his journey, which will end the same either way. Falling off the cliff represents the birth of a human being, and hitting the ground represents death. Clearly we can see that clinging and attaching in this situation does not do the man any good. It is the same when it comes to attachment in our own lives. We are all guilty of attachment – to ideas, beliefs, people, goals, and even attachment to life (fear of death). One thing that's important to understand is that attachment only leads to suffering. This universe is constantly changing in every way and in every moment. Nothing we attach to will last forever. We may attach and hold on as much as we want, but there really is nothing to hold onto. It is very foolish to attach. If we practice detachment, we can learn more, suffer less, and live a much more peaceful life.

To help understand attachment a little more, here is another story that comes from the book The Teaching of Buddha. In this story, there is a man who is traveling and eventually comes across a river. He needs to cross the river so he takes some time to build a raft to get across. Once he crosses, he thinks it's a good idea to keep the raft, should he ever need to use it again. This raft, like any other, is awkward to carry and quite heavy. You can understand how much effort this man is exerting to bring this raft with him on his journey. Attachment to anything in life, like the raft, is an unnecessary burden and we are much better off just going with the flow. Appreciating each part of life as it comes, and letting go when it's time to let go, is a critical skill when it comes to our learning and development. If we resist change and stubbornly attempt to keep things the same, we are only prolonging the inevitable.

01:
EVERYTHING
IS **ENERGY**

Think in terms of **energy**

One of the main foundational lessons to learn is that the universe and everything in the universe is energy. You would be lucky to find a scientist, physicist, or philosopher that doesn't believe everything is vibrational and everything is energy. Do the tiniest bit of research on this subject and we can easily find evidence to prove this. Energy can never be created or destroyed and energy is always moving. Objects that appear to be solid are constantly vibrating and changing. It's all happening at microscopic levels beyond what the naked eye can see. If we take a microscope and look at any solid object close enough, we can see that the tiniest particles all break down to vibrating energy. Everything we experience, see, hear, smell, taste, or touch is just the universe expressing itself in different forms of energy. Without energy, the sun wouldn't be shining, our hearts couldn't be beating, life on earth would not be flourishing, and the universe would cease to exist.

Energy is at the source of all creation, and creation is always happening. The universe is always happening, things are always changing, and nothing can stay the same forever. There is never a moment in time where creation takes a break. Creation is an ongoing phenomenon that has been happening, and continues to happen. There are so many studies, books, and documentaries focused around this idea that everything is energy. Yet there are still so many people living in the dark or who just do not understand the importance of this truth.

As humans, we have a deep connection with energy. We have the ability to sense and manipulate energy, and one of the ways we do so is with our awareness. Our awareness allows us to move into different parts of the mind, which causes us to feel certain feelings and think certain thoughts. With this ability, we work in cooperation with the universe to create or allow every experience into our lives, whether we are doing so consciously or unconsciously.

Consider for a moment all of the things that humans have created using awareness, the manipulation of energy, along with the cooperation of the universe. Houses, cars, planes, trains, technology in general, politics, religions, languages. All of these creations had to first exist in our mind as thought or idea before appearing into reality. That goes for anything that humans have created. These thoughts are energy, and scientists can literally measure our thoughts because of the energy involved. We humans have the ability to create anything, using just our minds and energy. Consider all the things that you personally have created in your own life: experiences, relationships, life events, goals achieved. All creation is relatively the same process and once we begin to understand this process and how it works, we can start using it to our advantage.

"We can do anything if we put our mind to it" - Khalid

The universe expresses its energy in many different ways. We see the sun shining, water flowing, trees growing, shooting stars, humans, animals, etc. As humans, we express our energy through our thoughts, emotions, and actions. These three components are the main factors that work together to create one overall energetic vibration that each person emits in every moment. These are the "good vibes" and the "bad vibes" we get when we spend time around other people, and those we feel when we are by ourselves too. It's all just energy flowing through us.

Keep in mind, this energy cannot always be controlled – but it can be managed.

We have the ability to use our willpower or our awareness to create and sustain our own vibration at any moment. We also have the ability to become aware of our vibration at any moment, which allows us to overcome and change our vibration whenever we want. In other words, we can think whatever we choose to think, feel whatever we choose to feel, do whatever we choose to do, be any kind of person we want to be, and believe whatever we choose to believe. The key point that most people do not realize is that our vibration has a direct impact on the entire chemistry of our body, as well as the universe around us. Research has shown us that stress can seriously damage our mind and our body and is one of the main causes of disease and illness. It makes sense because if someone is constantly in a state of bad vibrations, they are destined to attract bad things into their lives and make it nearly impossible to attract good things.

In our relationship with the universe, the role of the universe is to match our vibrations/energy and echo the same vibrations/energy back to us as experiences, events, impulses, thoughts, and emotions. When we get on a vibrational level and sustain it, the universe will return that vibration and show us exactly what kind of vibration we have been giving off. In other words, we must give (vibrationally) before we can receive or manifest our desires into physical reality. Understanding this will help us understand why we may not always get what we want. We do, however, always get what we deserve, and we get what we are ready for on a level of energy and vibration. All energy that comes through us is borrowed from the universe and must be returned eventually. The contrast is also true: we let the universe borrow our energy and we can trust the universe will give back the same energy we gave off originally.

By understanding our awareness and the universe, we can learn to concentrate and focus our energy in ways that will benefit our overall vibration. A wise monk named Dandapani describes our awareness as a glowing ball of light. We have the ability to take our awareness and move it into any part of our mind we choose. Wherever our awareness is present, that part of our mind glows and begins to build up energy.

This creative process of focusing energy is a skill that can be practiced, improved, and forgotten if we don't practice it daily. Like with any skill, persistence and patience are the two main components to mastering this skill. Before getting into the specifics on how exactly this skill can be practiced, it is critically important to understand the facts about ourselves and the universe. Deliberately creating without understanding the facts of creation and energy is like playing a game without ever learning the rules. We are much better off preparing ourselves in advance and learning the game before we fully jump into it, and we will be much better at the game compared to someone who does not understand the rules.

We are always giving off some sort of vibration at any given moment in time. Regardless of what we are giving off, there are only two directions we could possibly be headed, which simplifies the process. Vibrationally, we are either headed toward our desires or away from them. That is the key. If we are ever curious as to which direction we are headed, we can just ask ourselves, "Are my thoughts and feelings aligned with my desires or are they going against my desires?" In other words, are you feeling good about your desires or are you feeling bad? Although the answer to this question may not always be clear, it sure can be a great way to put ourselves back on track and correct our thinking. If you are feeling bad, that just means you might be doing something wrong or headed in the wrong direction. The key there is to try something new, look at things from a different perspective, and try to think positive, if possible.

Thankfully, there is a time delay in our vibration, so we will not always attract the same vibration back to us instantaneously. This eliminates any fear or worry about not being in the right state of mind. It happens to the best of us and when it does, it is best to just let it be rather than resisting it. Without a time delay, we probably would be killed with all the negative thoughts and emotions that we give off on a daily basis. The time delay is one thing that stumps many people. As humans, we tend to become impatient and want our dreams to come true right now, but that's not how creation works. Time heals everything and it always takes time to create something new. You might have heard the saying, "Rome was not built in a day," and this just goes to show you that creation must take time, especially a creation as massive as Rome. If there is one thing that's for sure, it's that we can trust the universe to do its job and return our vibrations to us. Our job is not to decide who, when, where, or how the vibrations will return to us. Our job is to decide what vibration we want and why we want it, and then offer that vibration as often as possible. As far as vibrations go, the universe will take care of the rest. Even when things might seem like they are going wrong, we can still trust that the universe is on our side and everything that is happening will bring some sort of benefit or life lesson to us in due time.

Alan Watts, a British theologian and philosopher, described it beautifully when he said the relationship between humans and the universe is transactional. Just like buying and selling, the act of selling cannot exist without the simultaneous act of buying. In the same way, buying could not exist without the simultaneous act of selling. With humans and the universe, all transactions involve this exchange of energy. We cannot expect to give away energy without getting some kind of energy back.

If our awareness is focused on something, consciously or unconsciously, we give our energy to it. Anything we focus on grows, so if we do not desire to see something grow, we must refocus our energy on something we do want to see grow. Usually we can take what we do not want and look at the exact opposite to find out what we do want. By redirecting our energy and focusing on what we do want, we can begin to move in a more beneficial direction vibrationally. Energy flows where attention goes, and what we resist persists. So do not resist the things that we do not desire; simply surrender, let go of undesirable energy because it does not serve us, and allow any better feeling thoughts into our awareness to keep our vibration high. This is easier said than done, and we can't always control every thought we have, and that is why we have meditation, which will be discussed later in the book.

Yes, this means that being mindful and aware of our thoughts and feelings is extremely important in the creative process. We have the ability to choose any vibration we want to offer and, whatever we offer, we will attract more of that into our life. If we notice ourselves giving off a vibration that is not desirable, it's not the end of the world. We need negative vibrations to help us recognize and appreciate positive vibrations, so be thankful any time the vibration becomes clear, whether we view it as good or bad.

Wayne Dyer, mentioned earlier, also has a great understanding of how our thoughts affect our reality. In one of his talks, he says, "Anything that divides us weakens us. Any thought that you have that divides you from somebody else, that makes you better than somebody else, any judgmental thought at all is not a thought of source and the minute you leave source, you lose the power to manifest. You lose the power to attract into your life what you want. Any thought that unites us, that includes us, that is of service, any thought of spirit and spiritually that brings us together as one and recognizes the truth that all of us have come from the same source... strengthens us and gives us more power to manifest our desires." This is a very powerful message to those who can understand it and apply it in everyday life. Before you judge someone or before you try to wish harm upon someone else, remember that you will pay the price and trust me, it's not worth it.

Our thoughts or our overall vibration is not something that can be controlled; rather, it is something that can only be managed. Attempting to maintain control of anything only creates resistance. Just like in nature, our lives are all unfolding naturally before us, one moment at a time, and nature is not something that can be controlled. Everything that we experience is something that we have allowed into our lives based on the vibrations we have been offering in the past or the habits that we have developed, or it is a lesson that we need to learn. We cannot feel anger unless we allow ourselves to feel angry, or unless we have not yet learned to cope with anger. The same goes for feeling happy or any other emotion. We cannot force ourselves to be happy when we're angry, nor can we force ourselves to be angry when we are happy. We can, however, manage and be aware of the struggle taking place in our mind. By doing this, we can eventually transcend that struggle. The same goes for attracting any desire into our lives. Let's take attracting a lover for example. We cannot force someone to love us and we cannot force ourselves to love someone else. We must first offer vibrations of love to ourselves and by doing so, we can then allow our love to reach others naturally. From there, we can begin to attract love to flow our way from all around us.

Another important thing to understand about energy is that it builds momentum, sometimes very quickly, and this is why what we focus on grows. The more we can focus on a vibration, the more momentum it will build up, and the harder it will be to stop once it gets going. Just like a snowball rolling down a mountain turning into an avalanche. Let's look at an example. If I am thinking about a situation that made me upset, the longer I think about it, the more thoughts I will build up around that subject. The more thoughts I create around the subject, the more likely I am to experience feelings or emotions similar to those thoughts. If I continue to allow these thoughts and feelings into my life, I will eventually gain enough momentum to take a negative action based on my thoughts and feelings. The action that I take is a result of all the momentum that has accumulated. That action could be prevented if the momentum had been stopped earlier. There comes a point where it seems impossible to turn back because of all the momentum built up. If we can learn to recognize negative energy and learn to let go of it, we can stop it from building momentum. Once it gains momentum, it's going to have an influence on our environment. This also means that positive energy and positive vibrations build momentum the same way. If you can reach a certain vibration, sustain it for long enough, and continually find a way to return to it, there will be a point where you become unstoppable. No matter what gets in your way, you can break through it and keep going in the direction of creating your desires because of the momentum that has been built up.

The universe is very forgiving when it comes to the vibrations we offer. If we offer an undesirable vibration for, say, ten minutes, recognize it, let go of it, and then allow a more desirable vibration to come into existence, we will, more than likely, not have to experience the undesirable vibration echoing back to us. Even if we have been offering an undesirable vibration our entire lives, the universe will allow us to change our vibration, which will change the course of our lives. The universe does not hold grudges, and if we hold grudges or let ourselves be unforgiving, we create our own resistance and a negative vibration for ourselves, which will only be a hindrance when it comes to creating a desirable life.

"Everything is relative." - Albert Einstein

Everything in this universe is relative; this is one of the most important lessons we can learn. The human being needs the universe just as much as the universe needs the human being. Without the human being, there would not be a perspective of the universe because we experience the universe from a human point of view, and without the universe, we wouldn't have the ground to stand on, air to breathe, or anything to sustain life for us. One simply cannot exist without the other. In the same way, hard cannot exist without soft, light cannot exist without darkness, hot cannot exist without cold, male cannot exist without female, pleasure cannot exist without pain, life cannot exist without death. It may come off a bit silly quoting **The Lion King,** but it's true when Mufasa tells Simba, "Everything you see exists together in a delicate balance. As King, you need to understand that balance and respect all creatures."

Let's take just one of these examples and look further into it. If there were no such thing as pain and there was only pleasure, pleasure could not exist. The only reason why a human being would consider something to be pleasurable is because we have something painful as a comparison. If there were nothing painful to compare it to and pleasure existed by itself all the time, then it wouldn't be pleasurable. The opposite is also true. Let's say that life only consisted of pain and no pleasure. The only reason why we have pain is because, in relation to something pleasurable, it is painful.

Now what does relativity mean and why is this important? What this really means is that the two opposites that are in relationships with each other are actually the same thing. They are connected in such a way that they are absolutely dependent on each other. They exist perfectly enough to balance eachother out. They are the same thing, just multiple different components working together to create one unified whole. Pain/pleasure are one thing, hot/cold are one thing, the universe/humans are one thing. Another good example is a coin. A coin has a heads side and a tails side. You couldn't have a coin with just one side. Each side of the coin must exist in order for the coin to exist at all.

To make things even more clear, the universe can be considered as anything and everything that exists or has ever existed, whether that be physical or non-physical. Many people have the misconception that the human being and the universe are separate, but a human being is not an organism in an environment; the human being is an organism/environment. Alan Watts describes us as a unified field of behavior. If we carefully describe any behavior of any organism, we cannot do so without also describing the behavior of the environment. We are really describing the behavior of a unified field, meaning that us as humans and our surroundings are one in the same. An organism is not the puppet of the universe, nor is the universe a puppet of an organism.

In addition to our relationship with the universe as a whole, we have relationships with many individual parts of the universe. One of the most common relationships we come in contact with is our relationship with our circumstances and things that are going on in our lives. We even have a relationship with our emotions and our thoughts. Many of us tend to avoid or reject circumstances, events, thoughts, or emotions that we don't like and this rejection only creates resistance. There is no way to get rid of these negative situations in our lives; they are a part of our life just as much as positive situations, so what we can do is accept all circumstances and just view them in a different way. If we can become friends with the positives and negatives, embrace them, and learn to live with them, instead of trying to do the impossible and get rid of them, we will have a much more pleasant experience on this earth.

Many of the most successful modern-day music artists, such as Drake, definitely understand many of these lessons about the universe. I believe that understanding these fundamental lessons is the reason why anyone sees success in their life or career. One of Drake's lyrics goes, "What have I learned since getting rich, yeah I learned working with the negatives could make for better pictures." So, instead of ignoring the negatives or being afraid of them, we can work with them and use them to make better pictures in all situations.

The simple idea of thinking in terms of positive and negative energy is such an amazing technique to use if we want to better manage our vibration. With a better understanding of energy, we gain a better understanding of ourselves and the universe. Keeping energy in mind at all times, we can start making better decisions with our energy – and when we do, the rewards are priceless.

02: **CHOICE**

My life is **my choice**

The human being is a very complex species and most of us have so much going on in our lives that we don't ever take the time to learn about ourselves. Most people are so caught up in the game of life that we forget that we are more than just an animal trying to survive. We have so much potential, so much power and we can thrive in all areas of life, if only we realize our true potential. Many people are searching for answers outside of themselves and searching for valuables outside of themselves hoping to experience pleasure, but the most valuable things in life are really our mind, body, and spirit – the things that were given to us for free, the things that we were born with, the things we die with - And all of these valuables can be experienced and understood by searching inside of ourselves.

One trait we have as a human being, which is completely free, is the ability to choose and have preferences. We choose what we want to focus on. We choose which voice in our head we want to pay attention to. We choose, and we pay the price for our choices, or we reap the rewards of our choices. We choose what kind of foods, music, people, habits, and experiences we have in our lives. This ability to choose is the reason why we don't all like the same things and we don't all desire the same life or experiences. It's the reason why we make poor choices, and the reason why we make wise ones. It's the reason why some people stay the same, and some people change. We use this ability all day every day and it is very powerful and important to understand that we always have a choice, in everything we do. We may sometimes run into a situation where our only choices are both painful and undesirable, but in these cases or in any case, we can only choose the path of least resistance. The path of least resistance may not always be clear, but it's the same as finding the path of most pleasure. You know what you want, your job is to choose. The universe will then do its job and lead you to where you need to be in life. Any path that is chosen is the right path for our own personal growth. So there is no need to contemplate our past decisions, wondering if they were wrong or right. If you learned a lesson and if you can move forward from that lesson, then you made the right choice.

As humans, we have the ability to choose to stop growing and stop changing. Of course we all physically grow old, but growing and changing in terms of what's inside us. Some people choose beliefs and preferences when they are young and resist change for the rest of their lives, even if the change could benefit them and/or the people around them. These are the kinds of people who often might refuse to use technology and claim they're "old-fashioned." The same type of people may hold grudges for years, or stay angry at a person/event in their past until their deathbed. These are just a few examples of people resisting change who could simplify and improve their lives with just one easy choice. Also, as mentioned earlier, when you choose to stop changing, and choose to stay the same, you cut yourself off from learning, growing, or moving forward in life, which is essential to our evolution.

With this trait of choice (some may call it free will), something else we can do is learn to choose our reaction to anything that is happening around us. When it comes to reacting, we are either doing one of two things. We are allowing the environment to influence us and our reaction, or we are creating our own reaction that will influence the environment around us. We cannot necessarily choose everything that comes into our lives at every moment, but we can choose how we react to the things that come into our lives. The more we recognize our reactions and choose reactions that serve us, the easier it becomes.

I've worked in the customer service industry for many years, and even outside of that, I have experienced many people who have come into my life and expressed their negative energy to me. As soon as I learned that I could choose my reaction, I began to realize that without a negative reaction, their negativity is powerless. Nobody can make you feel bad unless you also allow yourself to feel bad. Whether you are dealing with people, or some other negative situation in your life, you always have a choice to how you react, and how you choose to react will determine your reality in that moment.

There will be times when old habits will get the best of us or where we let our guard down and make a mistake. Also, remember that it is okay to feel bad sometimes. It happens to everybody and when it does happen, let it happen, accept it, and move on. Everybody makes mistakes, so don't beat yourself up if you make one. Take mistakes as lessons and use them to move forward rather than backwards. Earl Nightingale once said on one of his records, "The only people who never make mistakes are the ones who never try anything."

Habits are also a huge factor in creation. Many people do not understand that we can create or get rid of habits by choice. As humans, just like any other living creature, we are naturally habitual creatures. Some habits may serve us and benefit us while other habits may hinder us and be destructive to us and our future. We can have habits of vibration (awareness, thought, feeling, and emotion) and we can also have habits of action and reaction. All habits directly affect our vibration and affect what we attract into our lives.

If we want to know what our future looks like, we can first take a look at our daily habits. This is to say that our habits are shaping and molding our lives and our future. Most things we do on a daily basis are habitual because most people are typically doing the same thing every day like working, going to school, eating, using the bathroom, etc. Going back to momentum, any habit starts out as something small or something as simple as a single thought, and builds momentum to a point where it happens without even thinking about it.

This habitual way of being and the way momentum is built into our thoughts and actions is the same way that beliefs are created in our life. A belief is a thought that is repeated and usually analyzed over and over until it becomes part of our habitual programming. Beliefs are perhaps the most important factor in creation. Not only do we have the ability to choose our habits, we also have the ability to choose what we believe. At a young age, when our beliefs are not fully developed, it is much easier to program beliefs, but regardless of age, we can still change our beliefs if we desire to do so. Beliefs, like habits, can either hinder us from reaching our true infinite potential, or they can benefit us tremendously and move us forward. So how do we change a belief? First, identify a belief that you want to change, or identify a belief that you want to create. Then think of a beneficial belief and repeat that thought over and over until it becomes habitual and then boom! – you've got a new belief. This may take a few days or weeks but regardless, it can be that simple. During that process, you will recognize that evidence to support the new belief will start entering into your life, and things get much easier from that point.

A great example of beliefs holding us back is the story of Roger Bannister and the four-minute mile. There was a point in time where people really believed a four-minute mile could not be achieved by humans. A Harvard Business Review article quotes, "Several theorists proclaimed it was impossible physiologically for humans." People had been trying to accomplish this impossible task since at least 1886 and one day in 1954, Bannister finally broke through that illusion and beat the four-minute mile. Forty-six days later, a man named John Landy broke the record again. Within the next year, three more runners broke the same barrier. This just goes to show us how humans individually, and as a group or entire species, can have limiting beliefs that interfere with our way of achieving our true potential. Bannister made the choice to believe that he could achieve something that other people thought was impossible. The people who truly believe and realize our limitless potential are set free and can begin creating new realities for themselves and the whole world.

One other factor that may be holding us back from making choices that will help us move forward with creation is our perspective – the way we view the world around us. Isn't it interesting that two people can look at the exact same thing and see two completely different things? In my opinion, there are two general ways of looking at things. The Optimist, who will look out the window and watch the rain fall and think of how beautiful nature is, and the Pessimist, who will look out the window, miss the beauty of nature, and only think of how the sun is gone and the rain is ugly. Every person has a different belief system, background, and personality that molds our own perspectives. No matter the perspective, it can and will change over time, and we should remember that we have the choice to change that at any moment. If we change our perspective, we can change our beliefs. The opposite is also true. If we can change our beliefs, we can change our perspective of the world. Our perspective can make or break any person when it comes to the creative process, and our perspective will determine how we experience each day.

There's an old saying by writer Anaïs Nin: "We don't see things as they are, we see things as we are." This is the same idea that if we look at something in nature and view it as ugly, it's not really that way – we just have an ugly point of view.

One question I've learned to ask myself when thinking in terms of perspective is: Is this the best way to look at things? If we think about our surroundings or our situation, using that question tends to help us change perspectives pretty quickly and for the better.

Changing perspectives and beliefs involves an understanding of where our original perspectives and beliefs come from. In 2013, neuroscientists at Emory University did an experiment on mice showing how beliefs could actually be passed down from generation to generation. This means not only do we have our own negative limiting beliefs holding us back from our infinite potential, but we also have our parents' and our grandparents' beliefs potentially holding us back as well.

The experiment placed two groups of mice in fixed environments. The first group was simultaneously exposed to a particular odor and a variable that would produce fear. Another group of mice was exposed to the same odor without any fear variable. When the next generation was born, mice from each group were exposed to the same odor. Despite never having been exposed to any real fear variable, the second generation of mice from the first group would actually have the same fear response as the older generation simply because of the environmental factor posing no real threat at that moment. The second group of mice was exposed to the same odor and, like the generation before, had no reaction.

There are many factors that affect our beliefs and our perspective but what it all comes down to is that we have the ability to change our beliefs and perspective by changing our thoughts. The more we can recognize our limiting thoughts behind our limiting beliefs and perspectives, the more we can work on changing them to evolve toward the best version of ourselves. In 2018, I was fortunate enough to see John Maxwell speak in person through a business event. Maxwell is an American author, speaker, and pastor who is very successful in his career. During his speech, he said, "How we view things determines how we do things" and "What I believe about life determines how I perceive life which determines what I receive from life."

Whatever we believe to be true will prompt the universe to bring us more evidence to support our beliefs. Our beliefs hold a specific vibration that we give off any time that belief is active, and anything we give must be returned to us. Our beliefs and perspectives are based on what we focus on frequently and persistently. We live in a day and age where many people spend time daily watching TV, listening to music, or staring at their phones. This is where many beliefs and perspectives are shaped for the majority of us.

Someone who watches the daily news, for example, may be exposed to an excessive amount of negativity such as crimes, tragedies, and natural disasters, which can easily influence that person to believe that the world is a dangerous place full of terrible things. This will prompt the universe to draw your attention toward many more circumstances and events that support the belief that the world is a dangerous place. At the same time, this causes the universe to create more circumstances and events around that person to confirm that belief even more than it was before. Every other belief, thought, and action that occurs in our daily life has the same effect on us, and the universe around us.

Music can also have a huge influence on our beliefs and perspectives of the world, especially in the moment where we are listening it. For example, if a person listens to music every day that delivers a message about heartbreak and loneliness, it makes sense that that person is very likely to feel and experience heartbreak and loneliness. On the other hand, if someone listens to music that conveys a message about being strong, confident, and brave, that person may more likely feel strong, confident, and brave. This just seems like common sense, but so many of us still choose to stick with what we know, and listen to music that doesn't benefit us. Music is a powerful manipulation tool and when we listen to it, we are subconsciously allowing that artist's message to flow through us. If we listen to the same type of music enough, it can very well play a huge factor in determining our main beliefs. We choose what we pay attention to on a daily basis, so let's make the wise decision and focus our energy on things that will benefit us and the world around us.

One of the most powerful phrases that relates to beliefs/perspective is "I am." Many religions understand that "I am" is very powerful and what comes after that phrase can very well determine our future in many cases. This is one simple way to start recognizing or changing some beliefs that may be harming us. Here are some examples of "I am" beliefs that may be hindering our ability to create:

I am not good enough
I am too old/young
I am too short/tall
I am too fat/skinny
I am lazy
I am ugly
I am forgetful
I am afraid
I am worried
I am scared
I am accident prone
I am weak
I am alone
I am busy
I am powerless

Here are some examples of "I am" statements that we can say to ourselves instead of using the limiting "I am" statements. These phrases may help us in our ability to evolve rather than hindering us:

I am honest
I am worthy
I am brave
I am strong
I am learning
I am kind
I am loving
I am accepting
I am caring
I am helpful
I am beautiful
I am improving
I am a creator
I am the master of my thoughts
I am limitless
I am forgiving
I am trusting
I am patient
I am unstoppable
I am ready

You may have noticed that each of these phrases sets off a different vibration as you read them, but clearly there are certain "I am" phrases that benefit us and those that hurt us. This is also true with all of our beliefs, habits, thoughts, feelings, and actions.

Even if you really do believe that you identify with the negative "I am" phrases, that just means that in the past, up until this moment in time, you have identified with those phrases. In this moment now, you can choose to quit identifying yourself with the limiting beliefs and start choosing those that empower. Your beliefs about yourself can and will change your life. It is absolutely necessary to form positive beliefs about ourselves if we wish to create the life we desire.

The "I am" phrases are also great examples of the power of the spoken word. The words that we speak and the story that we tell about ourselves says a lot about our vibration, our beliefs, and our relationship to the universe, especially "I am" phrases. Anything that comes after "I am" tends to be one of our strongest beliefs; otherwise, we wouldn't be saying it.

Listen to the words that you speak. Listen to the message you are sending to the universe and to other people. By doing this, we can easily recognize if something is off in our vibration. For example, if we feel the urge to complain, or communicate pain or suffering or anxiety, we are giving off a vibration that is going to attract more complaints, pain, suffering, and anxiety.

These negative vibrations we give off cause the people around us to feel the same vibration, unless they are very in tune with their own individual vibration. Instead, speak of appreciation, or something that feels good. Instead of always finding something to complain about, find something to be grateful for. This will also provide positive energy for ourselves and the people around us, meaning more things to be grateful for will be attracted to our lives.

Some classic common examples of spoken words that we may want to avoid are phrases like:

"I only spill food on myself when I'm wearing white."
"I guess today is just one of those bad days."
"I always mess things up."
"With my luck, something bad will probably happen."
"I can't help it, I've always been this way."
"I can't change."
"This disease runs in my family so I will probably have it too."

Anything that we speak about frequently, or speak about with strong conviction, is very likely to be attracted back to us in our reality. One thing that we should never do is discuss our diseases or disorders with other people, unless it's a doctor or someone who can actually help. Speaking of an existing disease does nothing other than spread negative energy and will have no benefit to anyone. A classic example is someone who breaks their arm. This person may talk about their experience, going into extreme detail, so much that the people listening actually cringe and imagine what it would be like to have the same thing happen to them. It is natural for people to empathize, so do yourself and everyone else a favor and leave the pain and suffering conversations at the door to prevent them from spreading. By being aware and changing the things we talk about, we can take a surprisingly significant leap toward our desires and raise our average vibration.

We should also be aware that when we speak about our desires, we are telling others how strongly we believe in that desire. I like to use the example: When I get a Ferrari vs. If I get a Ferrari. This is just one way of showing how we could be holding ourselves back from our own manifestations just by the words that come out of our mouth. If you catch yourself saying "if I ever" rather than "when I", it would be a good idea to correct yourself immediately as well as moving forward. One phrase shows a lack of confidence, and more of a wish that we hope will one day come true. The other shows a goal or a plan. It shows that we believe in creating this in our lives and that it's only a matter of time. It should be easy to tell which is more beneficial.

In the 1937 book, *Think and Grow Rich* by Napoleon Hill, there are timeless pieces of information that refer to a similar way of looking at our goals. In his book, he says "There is a difference between wishing for a thing and being ready to receive it. No one is ready for a thing until he believes he can acquire it. The state of mind must be belief, not mere hope or wish. Open-mindedness is essential for belief. Close minds do not inspire faith, courage, and belief". With that being said, pay close attention to everything that comes out of your mouth. If we never recognize our limiting beliefs, we won't ever change them.

A similar way of thinking is applied when we are speaking about the difficulty of a task. If you go into a task believing it is going to be very difficult, that belief alone is going to make the task extremely difficult for you. The opposite is also true. Heading into a task with the belief that it will be easy is not always the wisest decision to make, but have confidence that even if you are facing a tough task, you can learn quickly and adapt to achieve the desired results.

Another mistake many of us make with our words is arguing for our limitations or making excuses. Arguing for limitations usually happens in a situation where we have messed up somehow and are being corrected by someone or attempting to correct ourselves. If we make a mistake, there is no need to argue for our limitations and explain why we didn't do things right. There is no benefit that comes from excuses, and in many cases there is no benefit that comes from apologizing. All of these reactions focus our energy toward the wrongdoing. What we can choose to do instead is to learn from our mistakes and attempt to improve in that moment or the next time around. Focus on the lesson learned and the changes we wish to see, not the mistake or problem. If we keep the problem active in our vibration, the problem will surely stick around and reintroduce itself in the future, and the solution will wait for our mindset and actions to change.

A good example of arguing for limitations could be something as simple as a child who gets in trouble for drawing on the wall with a permanent marker. The child could say, "But I didn't know it was wrong" or "I was just trying to draw and have fun, I didn't know" or the child could say, "Okay, I won't do it again, I'll draw on paper from now on." I still catch myself arguing for my mistakes or my limitations at times, so just be aware when it happens and focus more on the solution rather than the problem.

Although the power of the spoken word may be great, the power of real action can be even more powerful. The combination of the two is even better. In John Maxwell's book, Developing the Leader within You 2.0, he shares a nice quote from Arthur Gordon: "Nothing is easier than saying words. Nothing is harder than living them, day after day. What you promise today must be renewed and re-decided tomorrow and each day that stretches out before you."

If we make promises to ourselves or other people and if we really intend to keep those promises, the best way to make that happen is to do like Gordon says: renew and re-decide, every day. Make the choice to do what is right. Starting any new habit may not always be easy. Setting goals and staying on track is no simple feat either. It takes constant and continuous discipline, willpower, and effort, which is one reason why many people resist changing or setting big goals. At the end of the day, we still have a choice. Do we want to stay the same or do we want to start moving toward the best version of ourselves and live our best life?

If we can understand the fact that we all have the ability to choose our beliefs, our perspective, our words, and our habits, then we are one step closer to getting things going in our favor. Our choices determine our reality and when it comes to the life we are living, most people don't realize that we have a choice. Sure, there are some situations in life in which we have no choice or control, but the idea is to focus on the opposite. Focus on things we can manage and things we can choose. One of the most important things we can do is start making choices and decisions about our desires. By choosing what we want to create in life, we begin to activate the creative process in favor of our desires.

03: **DESIRE**

If you want it, you can have it,
but it comes **at a price**

When it comes down to it, the only reason we desire anything is because we desire the feeling we believe will come from what we desire after it's been manifested. If someone desires a relationship, for example, they don't necessarily desire another person or even the things they can do with that person; they really desire the feelings that can be felt as a result of a relationship being established. This feeling, just like any other, can be created intentionally without even being in a relationship. If we can dig deep into our own desires and figure out what we really want, we may realize that all we want is satisfaction in our outside physical reality and our internal reality. Once we finally accept and acknowledge this, we can begin to work toward obtaining our true desires starting from the inside out. Otherwise, we may never take the next logical step toward our desire: figuring out how to bring them into our reality.

One major mistake many people make in this process of turning desires into reality is waiting and expecting the environment to change and give us what we desire before we change our vibration to match our desires. In this situation, we may end up waiting forever. This has been commonly referred to as being a victim to the environment, meaning we allow the environment to have a significant impact on the way we feel or the way we think. Being manipulated by the environment is inevitable for many of us because there is so much in the environment that can bring us pleasure. Of course, in those pleasurable situations, we may want to allow the environment to change how we are feeling. We just need to be aware of when we are allowing this. Whether we are allowing the environment to bring us pleasure or suffering, we are giving it power to manipulate the way we are feeling. With that power, we must be prepared to suffer. We must take the good with the bad when it comes to environmental manipulation.

We need to become a vibrational match internally before we are able to create something in our outer reality. In other words, we need to feel like we already have what we desire in order to attract it into our life rather than waiting for the environment to change before experiencing the feeling. If we can internally and vibrationally change to match our desires, we can influence the environment to change and match our desires in ways beyond imagination.

By becoming a vibrational match to our desires, we move into that state of being ready to receive or being thankful. From that point we can begin to know and trust that we will attract our desires. There are many methods to become a vibrational match to our desires and we will go over those methods in the "Applying Knowledge" section of the book.

One thing we can always ask ourselves to see if we are letting the environment manipulate us is: Am I really feeling this way because of the situation or circumstance, or am I feeling this way because of how I am thinking of the situation or circumstance?

This is really something to think about because two people could be experiencing the exact same situation but one could be happy and the other miserable. Our feelings about any situation depend on the way we are thinking. From here we can typically awaken to the fact that we don't have to allow the environment to choose how we feel; we can choose for ourselves. Of course this takes practice, but that is what meditation and other methods are for.

To start thinking in the direction of our desires, we can start by finding and practicing gratitude. The feeling of gratitude in most cases can be much more powerful than the feeling of desire.

By choosing the vibration of gratitude, we become a magnet or an energetic vortex and begin drawing our desires into our lives. The more we feel grateful, the more we will attract things to be grateful for. This vibration is one of the easiest to access, simply because anything can be appreciated. Appreciation has everything to do with the way we are looking at things and has little to do with what we are actually looking at. Some things are easier to appreciate than others but it is possible to appreciate anything. If we can practice appreciating everything, we can easily practice appreciating things that we do not yet have in our lives. By appreciating things before we get them, we attract them into our lives even faster than we would by any other vibrational method. With this method, we also show the universe that we trust our process and we know that our desires are on the way. This is one method that has worked wonders for me personally and, like I said, it is one of the easiest to begin doing right away.

As the saying goes, "You don't know what you've got till it's gone." Many of us don't appreciate the little things in life until they are gone. By appreciating everything, we will know what we have and we will be able to get the best out of it before it's gone. Remember, nothing lasts forever, so appreciate everything while you still have it.

One of the most important things we can appreciate is ourselves. Many of us are very good at disciplining and punishing ourselves mentally when we do something wrong, but how many of us give ourselves props or appreciation when we do something right? Psychologically, this can be known as positive reinforcement. When I started practicing this in my own life, I immediately noticed a huge boost in self-confidence and motivation to do more good things. I would appreciate myself for simple things like making my bed, showing up to a meeting on time, eating healthy foods, remembering to get everything I need from the grocery store, cleaning up after myself, etc. I would appreciate myself as often as possible and actually tell myself "good job", and this alone has been one of the most rewarding mental exercises, along with trying to appreciate everything throughout each day.

One of the best things we can do to show appreciation to ourselves is to celebrate successes, big and small. We will talk about this later in the book, but by celebrating successes, we train ourselves psychologically to want to succeed more. Example: There's an employee at work who always goes above and beyond but never gets appreciation that they deserve. That employee is extremely likely to lower their performance because of the fact that they have nothing to gain by trying hard. However, if that employee were appreciated and their hard work celebrated somehow, they would be much more likely to continue working hard and doing well. We can do ourselves a favor and start celebrating every small success. If your goal is to eat healthier and you just ate vegetables for the first time in a month, go celebrate! If your goal is to stop watching TV and you are able to quit for one week straight, that's something to celebrate! The point is, appreciate where you are, and the small steps you take toward your goals.

Many religions have understood this idea of appreciation and being grateful for what we have. The Christian Bible has a quote: "For whoever has, to him more will be given; but whoever does not have, even what he does have will be taken away from him." (Matthew 12:13)

Chance the Rapper is a successful artist who also understands the power of gratitude. In one of his songs, he says, "When the praises go up, the blessings come down."

There will come a point when you have mastered the art of appreciation and that is when you can truly appreciate the pain and suffering of life. We've all slept somewhere uncomfortable before and know the feeling we get when we finally get back into our own bed after sleeping on the floor or couch. This feeling we get when the storm finally passes is a gift from the universe. Our bed would not feel so amazing if we did not ever get to sleep on the floor so if you were wise enough to see that future and know that the storm will pass, you could appreciate that storm. This is one thing that I am still getting the hang of: appreciating things I don't like.

Anyone can appreciate good things but it takes true wisdom and a vision of the future to appreciate pain and suffering. If someone were gifted a Lamborghini with $1,000,000 cash, it would be pretty easy to appreciate that. But who would appreciate a dump truck emptying their load on your front lawn and in your driveway? The appreciation master could find a way.

One of the main reasons why pain and suffering may show up over and over again in someone's life is because they haven't yet learned to appreciate it; instead, they resist, reject, and curse it. They fight with it and never let go. They avoid saying thank you to that person they detest, or that thing in their past, or that personal burden, and opt to resist instead. The resistance to pain and suffering is the very thing that causes the pain and suffering. Once we learn to appreciate these sorts of things, we are able to move toward actualizing our desires more swiftly.

We can view the vibration of our desires in one of two ways. There is the lack of our desire, or viewing our desires as something outside of us that we do not possess. Then there is a healthy or fulfilled desire that we are grateful to have. In other words, we can experience the vibration of what is wanted and be in harmony, or experience the absence of what is wanted – a vibration that will lead to greater suffering. Not all desire leads to suffering but if we do not know how to manage desire, we can easily slip into a low vibration, which will steer us away from our desires.

Any time we get angry or upset or sad for whatever reason, it is because we are projecting our energy toward the lack or absence of what is desired. By doing this, we are creating our own resistance and getting in our own way. We are cutting off our stream to abundance. As mentioned earlier, we can use the things we don't want to realize what we do want, and by making this transition, we can change our vibration. By changing vibration, we can change direction. We're always moving in one of two directions when it comes to our vibration. We are moving in a direction that will bring us closer to our desires or one that will take us away from our true passions.

Here are some simple ways to change direction just by switching from "not wanted" to "wanted" on a certain subject:

If we don't want war, we can focus on peace and leave war completely out of the picture.

If we don't want to end up like our parents, we can focus on how we do want to be in the future.

If we don't want to get in a car accident, we can focus on driving safely.

If we don't want to be scared, we can focus on being calm and brave.

If we don't want our significant other to leave us, we can focus on our significant other staying with us.

If we don't want debt, we can focus on increasing income.

If we don't want to fall down and lose our balance, we can focus on staying standing and keeping balance.

If we don't want to lose, we can focus on winning.

That last example is a powerful one that many people fail to understand. If we're focused on not losing, we are thinking defensively and we are thinking in a way that assumes loss will inevitably happen. It's very common to concoct ways to prevent certain things from happening – and what people don't realize is that tendency takes all of your energy away from winning and you often end up accomplishing nothing because all you can do is worry, plan, or prepare for the worst, rather than actually learning, growing, and working to achieve some kind of goal.

It's truly possible in any situation to find the path of least resistance and to choose the more comforting vibration that will lead us in the direction of our desires. The problem is that many people don't know the path is available or how to find it. It's not always going to be easy but the best way to do it is to practice recognizing vibrations regularly. Our feelings and our emotions act as indicators to let us know if we are on or off track from our desires. It takes a great amount of awareness and practice to be able to recognize our vibrations when they are off track. The awareness comes with time, patience, and persistence, just like anything we wish to create in our reality.

When we think of our desires and the fact that we can vibrationally have anything we truly desire, we start to realize two things. First, we can already have what we desire at this moment, and we don't need to search outside of ourselves for it. And second, we haven't thought about our desires enough to realize what we truly desire, which is just a better-feeling vibration.

As soon as we decide what we want in this life, and as soon as we make the decision that we are ready to sacrifice whatever it takes to get it, it's already ours. Discovering a want or desire is the very first step to creation. As long as we can keep a high vibration and take action when needed, we will attract all of the things we want. Childish Gambino says, "If you want it, you can have it, if you need it, we can make it, but stay woke." That's really all we have to do. The artist also says, "Keep all your dreams keep standing tall, if you are strong you cannot fall, there is a voice inside us all, so smile when you can." These are very powerful words. Giving up on our goals or desires will erase all the progress we've made and it becomes much more unlikely to witness that creation come to life.

It is our attitude toward the universe that determines the universe's attitude toward us. The easiest way to start this change is to focus on changing our attitude toward ourselves. If we approach a goal or a desire with the attitude that we will fail, the universe has no choice but to respond with a matching vibration, and we are more than likely to fail. The opposite is also true. If we approach a goal with the attitude that we will succeed and are willing to get up no matter how many times we fall down, we are more than likely to succeed because of our vibration of confidence that we are expressing to the universe.

A poor attitude will almost always get us into some kind of trouble. It will almost certainly lead us away from the potential manifestation we seek. If we look at any person regarded as successful and fulfilled, we will notice that person more often than not has a good positive attitude. Take a person who desires a promotion. If that person gives off an attitude and behaves like an average employee, that person will more than likely stay in that position. If that person changes his attitude and acts like a manager, that person will more than likely see a future in management. At the opposite end of the spectrum, we see the people who are unsuccessful, living in pain and poverty, and we will almost always find a negative attitude in that situation.

This idea of changing your attitude to match what you desire has also been referred to as "acting as if." We touched on this topic earlier when we said that the best way to manifest is to make changes internally before changes in the environment occur. This is the same idea. Earl Nightingale speaks of acting as the person we wish to become. By practicing this, we actually become that person. So whether it's applying for a job, auditioning for a play, applying for a loan, or talking to your crush, as long as we can act as if we know that we will have what we want, we eventually manifest that destiny.

"Acting as if" is perhaps one of the most powerful ways to actualize our desires. By doing so, we mix thought and emotion together to create a vibration of unstoppable potential. It has been mentioned in religious texts that by blending thought and emotion, we can move mountains, and "acting as if" is a great way to start. Science calls this process of melding thoughts and emotions a brain and heart coherence. By creating this coherence, we begin to unlock the full potential of human creation, now proven scientifically.

If we learn only one thing from all of this, let it be learned that by changing our attitude, we can change our lives. A poor attitude will get us nowhere in life, and a positive attitude will open doors we didn't know existed. Further, how we feel determines what we are wishing for, and nothing is more important than that right there because you will get whatever you consistently and persistently wish for.

There are many techniques we can use to create this brain and heart coherence. I like to refer to this method as creative visualization. The human mind is so powerful and complex that we can actually create any kind of imagery in our head with almost no effort. This imagery goes beyond visuals. We can imagine anything that corresponds to any of our senses. We can imagine an image of a basketball. We can imagine the taste of a lemon, the smell of coffee, the sound of an airplane, the sensation of warm sand on our feet. It's so simple to visualize, but many people neglect to exercise the imagination. Imagination and visualization are critical because anything that exists had to first be imagined. Imagination is the foundation of all human creation.

Visualization can become so real if we close our eyes and really focus on the feeling. When we have a goal or an intention in mind, the best thing to do is focus on the end product and really dig for the feelings that would come if the goal were to be completed. When using creative visualization, try to imagine everything you possibly can about the scenario you are wanting to create. What would it look like, smell like, taste like, feel like, sound like? The more detailed you can get with your visualization, the more real it will feel, and the easier it will be to "act as if" it's already done.

When I first started making my own goals, this visualization technique was something I practiced every night before bed and every morning when I woke up. Eventually I began visualizing at random times throughout the day, but when you're in bed with your eyes closed, it is much easier because there are usually no distractions. My visualizations became so powerful to the point where I would cry tears of joy and feel real feelings of excitement and happiness that I had rarely been able to feel ever before. If you have big goals like I do, then you can imagine what I'm talking about. Being able to experience reaching your goals before actually reaching them is the fuel we all need if we're going to stay on the path to our desires. These visualizations reshaped my personality and helped me understand that if I could create feelings and experiences like this inside of me, I could manifest something similar outside of me too.

The thing that most people do not know is that when we visualize something, our mind cannot actually distinguish what is real from what is imaginary. Dr. Joe

Dispenza performed a simple experiment to demonstrate this. He took a few groups of people and monitored their brain activity while performing a set of activities several days a week. He took the first group of people and had them play the piano with instructions several days a week for a few weeks. The second group fiddled around on the piano for the same amount of time but with no instructions. The third group didn't play the piano at all. Finally, the fourth group followed the same instructions as group one, except they visualized themselves playing the keys instead of actually doing it.

The results of this experiment showed that for group one, after practicing a set of instructions and learning how to play the piano, a new area of the brain lit up that had never been stimulated before. Group two had no new areas of the brain light up, simply because there were no instructions, so nothing was learned. The third group had the same results as group two. The fourth group that visualized themselves playing the piano had the exact same part of their brain light up as if they were really playing the piano, similar to group one.

There are many other experiments and tests out there that show this to be true. The main lesson to be learned is that when we visualize something, our mind doesn't know if it's a real-life event or a fabricated one. This is why, when we watch scary movies, we feel fear. Our mind actually thinks that what we are seeing is real, and because of that, produces the emotions and changes the entire chemistry of our body at that moment.

Visualization and imagination are important and helpful to us in the creative process because they allow us to see beyond the illusion of our current reality and instead sample some of the many infinite possibilities that lie ahead in our lives. This is also a skill that can be practiced and improved upon by continuous effort.

Nikola Tesla, one of the most brilliant visionaries in history, used the same kind of visualization techniques to design and perfect his own technology. This is pretty amazing, considering the fact that we still benefit from and use his work in today's modern electronic world. According to Tesla, "My method is different. I do not rush into actual work. When I get a new idea, I start at once building it up in my imagination, and make improvements and operate the device in my mind. When I have gone so far as to embody everything in my invention, every possible improvement I can think of, and when I see no fault anywhere, I put into concrete form the final product of my brain."

When it comes to the possibilities of the future, there is an infinite number and there will be many surprises in the long run. There is no way we can predict everything that will happen. If we did know, we would be living in the past. Time is a very interesting concept and a huge factor when it comes to creation. As human beings, we are all moving through reality in space time. If we want to go somewhere or do something, it takes time to move our body through space, and this is the same with everything physical in this universe.

The only real time that exists is the present moment. Even if we are thinking about the past or the future, we are doing so in the present. The present moment is where all of our energy is available to us and is the only place where we can put our energy to use. If we have a vision or desire for something in the future, we can only move toward it if we know what kind of movements and actions to be making right now in the present moment. Our mind can time-travel, but our body can only act in the present moment.

Many people think of time as seconds, minutes, hours, days, etc., but all of these are just units of measurement that we use as humans to help keep track of our movement through space. Even if there were no clocks or calendars, we would still continue on this infinite loop of energy moving through space just like all living things. Everything goes through seasons of change, but time is just an illusion. Of course time measurement is a convenience because we use it for maneuvering through space, such as when we meet up with someone. We would have a very difficult time seeing a person in space without also knowing when to meet them in time. Time is on our side as long as we are using the present moment to our advantage.

We can use the power of the present moment to capitalize on our desires. Desire is one of the most amazing traits we all have as humans, but it can also be the most dangerous. Alan Watts says, "The only reason why we suffer is because we desire," and if we look more into what he means by this, it can be very eye-opening. This should also help clarify the difference between good and bad desire, as mentioned earlier.

Someone who is hungry may suffer because they desire food. Someone who is feeling lonely may suffer because they desire another person or people. Someone who is impatient may suffer because they desire things to happen more quickly. Suffering happens when we focus on a desire as being something we don't have at that moment. Focusing on lack rather than fulfillment is what brings suffering.

Pleasure happens when we focus on a desire being fulfilled or when we focus on things we desire and already have, the same as being grateful.

This feeling that we get when we finally achieve our desires can be known as desirelessness. Think about it – the reason why we feel so good after we get what we desire is because we no longer desire it. We have released our desires and settled ourselves into the present moment, thus moving into a vibration of appreciation and gratefulness. When desire is gone, we no longer suffer. With desirelessness, we still have our personal preferences, wants, and desires, and we are accepting of any reality that comes our way, but we don't allow desire to create suffering. With desirelessness, we can raise our vibration to higher levels and use it as a tool to help us move toward our desires. It may seem contradictory, using desirelessness to achieve our desires, but it really does work.

The other factor that makes desire dangerous is that for nearly every desire, there is some sacrifice that must be made in order to manifest that desire. Making sacrifices does not always lead to suffering, but it's not always easy for us to give up something we love, even if we know it could benefit us. If we choose to take the creative path of desire in life, we must be willing and ready to surrender the good for the great, and we must be ready to make sacrifices.

I have been fortunate enough to speak with multiple successful business owners in person, who generate millions of dollars per year. One business owner, who asked to remain anonymous, mentioned how their line of business required lots of time away from the house, which meant giving up the idea of having a close family. Having a close family takes tremendous time and effort, and unless you are able to find work that allows for an abundance of free time, you will more than likely have to give up something similar. So regardless of what kind of desires we have in life, we absolutely must be willing to make sacrifices. You can have anything but you can't have everything. Desires come at a price, and in many cases we may have to give up something good in order to get something else that we consider to be better. Once I started applying this particular principle in my life, I began to use my time more wisely and substantially increased my productivity. I began giving up things I love to allow more free time for myself to do work that would bring me closer to my desires. This process of manifesting a desire may be tough sometimes, but it feels great to know that one day it will pay off.

That same business owner had a great point about the popular saying "Maybe it just wasn't meant to be." This business owner said, "That's BS" – if we want to make something happen, we have to be willing and ready to go over any speed bumps and remove any obstacles that may be in the way. If you experience failure, try again until you get it right. If you have the attitude of giving up or quitting early, you may never see the day where you are living your full potential and you may never manifest your true desires.

04: THE EGO AND **CONFORMITY**

I am more than **my ego**

Many of us may already know about the part of our personality known as the ego, but a good portion of the world's population still does not understand what it really is. The human ego is an idea that represents the way we appear to other people or the way we think we appear to other people. Because everyone has a different perspective, there are multiple different ways in which we can be viewed by others so every person we interact with usually shapes our ego for us as our lives evolve. Our ego tends to be a name that is given to us at birth by our parents and this ego is often mistaken as the true self. The ego is merely an idea or a thought about who we really are as a person, meaning it does not really exist in physical reality. It is something that is made up by ourselves and the people around us and it does not define the true version of us, although many people do choose to define themselves by their ego.

The ego is the voice in our head that cares strongly about what other people think of us. It is the voice that tells us to spend money on new clothes, even though we have plenty already. The ego is the part of us that wants to finance a brand new car when we have little to no money in the bank. The ego is the part of us that feels the need to be complicated or in sync with the rest of society. In reality, we can all be living a much more simple life without being so in sync. Our ego can interfere with our lives more than we realize it, and if we allow the ego to be the main voice in our head, it tends to steer us from the true path of least resistance. The idea is not to get rid of the ego completely but to understand the difference between the ego and the true self, and find a balance that works and benefits your individual lifestyle.

Sometimes the ego loves to stand out. Most of the time, the ego loves to fit in, be accepted, and compare itself to others. Conformity may be one of the main causes of the biggest problems in our society today. It involves people doing what everyone else is doing without really understanding why they're doing it, or people agreeing with the majority only because, well, it's the majority. Like many other living creatures, humans have a survival trait that recognizes patterns in human behavior, and when something is out of pattern or off track from the majority of people, we instinctively get a warning signal that sends us back to conforming because we think that is the way to survive. This is the same thing that birds have to help them stay with their flock. Humans were made to do way more than survive and when we look at the majority of the human population, that's really what many of us are doing – just surviving, going through the day-to-day life trying to get to the next day, the weekend, the next week, or next year. A small percentage of people on earth have the freedom to really live rather than just survive.

Many beliefs we have and words that come out of our mouths on a daily basis are a product of conformity. When we are young, we will repeat almost anything we hear someone else say and believe almost any statement someone tells us. As we grow older, most of us break away from lies and conformity, but many of us still carry beliefs and echo words that are simply unexamined assumptions, rather than self-actualized truths. Conforming to beliefs of the majority is something extremely simple, yet may cause a lifetime of self-destruction. There's a saying that goes, "The truth is still the truth, even if no one believes it. A lie is still a lie, even if everyone believes it." Many of us are living our lives with lies as our foundational beliefs, and we all should check ourselves and our beliefs often.

So far, only a small percentage of people in the world are able to recognize these truths about the universe. Those who are able to detach from conformity often end up living some of the richest and most freedom-filled lives imaginable. Clearly the majority of the world has not figured out how to become limitless and one of the main reasons is because we are all following in one another's footsteps, which can be beneficial, besides the fact that most of us don't know what we are doing or why we are doing it. Many people lack the ability to think and act independently because we simply have not established a strong enough relationship with ourselves and the universe.

Humans are made to be unique, stand out, and have our own personalities. So many people are caught up in the dance of conformity that the true self is often buried and tucked away for most of our lives. We all know that individuals with significant impacts on the world aren't cookie-cutter conformists. The greatest leaders and influencers are able to do so by straying from conformity and thinking outside the box. If we do what everyone else is doing, we will end up where everyone else is going. If we want to have more of a choice on where we end up in the future, we must be aware of conformity working in the world and be careful not to get sucked into its vortex.

Look at slavery. Slave owners thought it was acceptable just because everyone else was doing it. After years of slavery, thanks to rejecting conformity and many other reasons, they were able to realize that what they were doing was not right, and slavery was finally abolished.

We can see conformity working in many different areas of human nature, but one of the biggest sectors is religion. Religion is a touchy subject for most people because nobody wants beliefs forced upon them, or to be told their beliefs are wrong, which is completely understandable. The interesting thing is that most people as children are strongly encouraged to follow the same beliefs and religions as family, friends, or others. How many parents actually teach their children that they can choose their beliefs in an unbiased way? Most people are born into a religion and a certain belief system. Sure, most of us eventually cultivate our own beliefs and opinions but when it comes to religion, people usually don't wander far from the family. It's unlikely that a person would even take the time to learn about any other religion unless maybe stumbling across a class in school that teaches some of the basics about the world's religions. The idea of conformity around religion is so strong that one can easily become an outcast just by choosing to follow a religion or belief system outside of one's family.

Why are there so many different religions? Many people may have asked the same question at some point and most probably didn't find an answer unless they really looked hard. Most religions have very similar stories and teachings and all revolve around the same basic concepts like moral behavior and our relationship to a higher power. But can all of the stories and legends really be true? Of course they can. If we really think hard about this, we should be able to understand that all of these stories, religions, and teachings are meant to show and teach us the same basic lessons about life, just from different perspectives to fit with the different cultures and lifestyles of the world.

It makes sense to have some sort of personal relationship with our religion, but in reality, the relationship we are experiencing and building is universal regardless of what religion we follow. It's possible to have no religion and still build the same relationship just by understanding the lessons that religion has to offer and applying them in our everyday lives. We are all just building the relationship between ourselves and the world around us. This can also be known as a relationship to spirituality or a relationship to the universe.

The ego is really the only thing that is tying us to religion. Once we realize that, we can choose to break free from the conformity of religion if we wish to do so, and experience a whole new level of spiritual awakening. The ego is not the true self. The true self that can be labeled or described is not the true self. Someone who claims to know the true self is unreliable because to know the true self would require all of the knowledge in the universe. The only labels that could accurately describe the true self are "infinite" or "limitless."

This is not to say that people who label themselves as religious are doing anything wrong. They are actually doing things very right. Religion can teach many great lessons about family, community, relationships, trust, good morals, and many other important aspects of life. Not only that, but religion offers techniques and creates opportunities that allow people to raise their vibrations, alone or in groups, to attract more of their desires to them in their lives. As people living in this world of conformity, there may be pressure to actively participate in some sort of religion. As long as we know the truth about this relationship between us and the universe, we can potentially create the same and more benefits of religion in our daily lives without conforming to any religion.

In the Netflix series *Explained,* they mention that studies are showing how organized religions are becoming less popular while spirituality is becoming more popular among individuals. This could be related to the fact that many people are realizing and waking up to the truth of the universe, which is a very good sign.

Although conformity may seem like something to avoid, we can use conformity to our advantage. If we perform a good deed or respond to a situation in a peaceful and noble way, many people around will conform and pay it forward at that very moment or in the future. In the same way, by performing bad deeds or responding to situations in an abrupt or negative way, people are still likely to conform. Conformity is one thing that can always be recognized if we are looking for it. It happens everywhere in nature so it is natural for humans to do it. Clearly it can be either beneficial or harmful so it's important to be aware of it. If the leader of a pack of wolves is headed in the direction of danger, the pack will follow. If the leader heads in the direction of safety, the pack will also follow. Allowing ourselves to conform to anything in the environment is going to seriously influence our thoughts and actions and will have a tremendous impact on our lives, either positively or negatively.

Following trends is one of the easiest ways to get sucked into conformity, and the ego lives to follow trends. When we follow trends, we allow ourselves to conform to someone else's idea, which isn't always bad. In business, for example, following trends in the marketplace or trailing in the footsteps of another business who is successful may be a very profitable and wise decision. However, when it comes down to it, someone has to create the trends. The person creating the trends is the person who really understands the value of being unique. If we can be the bigger person and make the necessary changes before everyone else does, we can stay ahead of the game and keep ourselves out of the conformity that may hold us back. Don't wait for other people to change before you change. Make changes in your own life and become a better person and watch the people around you follow.

When I was first starting to understand the ego and conformity, I was hesitant at first because I knew I would lose the approval and support of many of the people I loved. This is one of the sacrifices that comes with a limitless lifestyle. When I finally made the decision to start thinking and acting outside the box, sure enough, I did lose some approval and support that my ego desired, but what I learned is that the people who really love you will support you no matter how ridiculous your goals or ideas may seem. The ones who don't support you don't deserve to be there in your life. It's definitely a tough pill to swallow but I can tell you that self-approval is worth way more than others' approval.

"I'd rather be hated for what I am than loved for what I'm not." - Russ (Russell Vitale)

My recommendation for each person is to be aware of the ego, be aware of conformity, and get to know the true self through meditation. Once you get to a point in life where you are fully connected with your true self, you can start working with the ego again if you wish. It would be a good idea to find a balance between the ego and the true self. Each person will have their own preference to how much they want to show their ego and how much they want to show their true self. Still keep in mind that the ego has a way of overcoming the true self if we allow it too often, so choose that balance wisely.

05:
MEDITATION
AND
MINDFULNESS

We become what
we think about

The main goal when it comes to manifesting our desires is to practice high vibrations and do what we can to stay on those good vibrations in each moment and throughout each day. In other words, be happy and feel good as often as possible. This practice of maintaining awareness of our vibration is often referred to as mindfulness in Buddhism. Buddha says, "Peace comes from within. Do not seek it without." The idea is not to search for pleasures outside of yourself, but rather to realize that pleasure is already inside of you and you don't have to do much to access it. We can raise our vibration by letting go of the thoughts, feelings, and beliefs that don't serve us, giving up the fight and the struggle, accepting what is, going with the flow, and fully allowing ourselves to be in the present moment.

If there is something in our mind causing great resistance and frustration, go with the flow and accept the vibration rather than resisting it. Keep it simple and think of the mind like water. If we imagine a stream of water running down a mountain, the water will eventually run into some obstacles such as a tree, log, rock, or hill. The water does not become frustrated at the obstacles, nor does it condemn or resist the obstacles for getting in its way or making things difficult. The water will accept any obstacle knowing that it is the earth's way of saying, "This is not the right way" and it will know and trust that there is another way around. Water will always take the path of least resistance. If we learn to be like water and trust that the obstacles in our lives are meant to be there as life's way of saying "Think differently" or "Try something else," then we can move forward and find peace like water does.

In the moments when we are reaching for a higher vibration, what can really help us is to know that we don't have to try or force anything. Experience will help us understand that trying or forcing our minds to do anything only creates resistance. The same is true when trying to force or control the environment; it only creates resistance. If we give up forcing and fighting, we allow ourselves to move into a place of calmness, peace, and bliss. This blissful feeling is the feeling we are striving for and it is the vibration that will attract our desires. It's not complicated. We can all begin as soon as today to make this one change in our lives and if we are consistent with the practice of letting go, we will surely be able to witness some life-changing results.

Our vibration may occasionally be difficult to manage, but it's helpful to understand that there is a vibrational scale that ranges from peace to depression. If we know where we stand on the scale, it may be easier to find our way back up to a higher vibration. Any time we are on the lower end of the vibrational scale, we are beginning to attract the things we don't want into our lives. The sooner we can move back up the vibrational scale, the sooner we can get back to attracting abundance.

Musical artist Sara Bareilles sings, "Don't stop trying to find me here amidst the chaos, though I know it's blinding there's a way out, say out loud, we will not give up on love now." To that end, no matter how low we may be in life or on the vibrational scale, there is a way out and the present moment holds the key to escaping our negative self.

If we look further into this vibrational scale, we will notice that all negative states come from being somewhere other than the present moment, or they involve a desire to control something that usually can't be controlled. Frustration, irritation, and impatience all take place when we desire something else to be happening other than what is going on in front of us. In other words, we are in a state of lack or hunger for something beyond our reach. We are resisting what is because of our own selfish desires. These desires can only be healed with time, patience, and persistence or simply letting go and accepting things the way they are at that moment. Worry and doubt creep in when our mind is so caught up in the future that we begin thinking of all possible worst-case scenarios. In these situations, we can take the opposite route and begin to think of best-case scenarios because both futures are potentially possible and there is no benefit of dwelling on uncertainties. Anger, rage, and hatred happen for similar reasons. The main point being, submit yourself to the present moment.

> *"If you are depressed you*
> *are living in the past.*
> *If you are anxious you are*
> *living in the future.*
> *If you are at peace you are*
> *living in the present."*
> *- Lao Tzu*

Many of us spend so much time in the past or the future that we completely miss out and take for granted all of the blessings we have in the present moment.

The present moment is where all creation happens. It's where ideas are birthed, actions are taken, and plans are made. Many scientists believe that the Big Bang is what created the universe and if this is true, it all happened in a present moment just like the one we are experiencing right now. The present moment is where all existence is happening and it's where all creations are made. If we can practice being in the present moment more often, it becomes simple to let go of worries, fears, and anxiety on command almost instantly. It's one thing to know and understand all of this intellectually, and it's another thing to actually experience it. True understanding comes from actual experience, and this is true in any situation for any skill, talent, or teaching. The intellectual understanding definitely helps but the experience is where everything starts to come together. To get the most out of this knowledge, the best thing to do would be to begin applying it immediately; otherwise, it can be easily forgotten.

Nassim Haramein, a world leader in unified physics, has spent more than 30 years researching and discovering connections in physics, mathematics, geometry, cosmology, quantum mechanics, biology, and chemistry, as well as anthropology and ancient civilizations. He has discovered some amazing equations that may help us better understand the universe. His thinking and his work is very similar to Albert Einstein's research on relativity and the universe. Nassim understands that we are all connected and all tapped into "universal consciousness" and he knows the key to understanding the universe. In one of his talks, he says in reference to universal consciousness:

> *You can increase the amount of information flow. You can increase your influence on the structure of space... if you become aware that you have that ability that you can connect with the space. So how would you do that? Well, every proton in the nucleus of every one of your atoms, and you're made out of one hundred trillion cells, each cell is made out of one hundred trillion atoms so there's a lot of those little guys, It's very advanced it's very complex, it's remarkable, there's a miracle happening every billionth of a second in your body... So all this is happening and each proton is connected to all other protons in the universe. All the information in the universe is present in each one. So if you actually want to know about the universe, where do you go? Inside yourself. We are constantly putting our attention outside ourselves because that's what we learn to do, but there are other techniques to*

help you bring your consciousness inside yourself and if you do that, you can get more and more conscious of the deeper layers of your existence because you think of yourself as one thing but you're made of all these billion trillions of things, and if you become aware of them, if you go deeper and deeper in them, eventually you can get a deeper level of information about the rest of the universe, like the root of you... which is much deeper than the personality and everything else that you've developed throughout the years.

So clearly we have a lot to discover about the universe and so many wise people have told us that we must search within ourselves, and becoming present in this moment is the way to begin this process. This is practiced in many ways and one very common method to practice being in the moment is meditation.

Alan Watts has a great way of describing meditation. He says:

"If I think all the time, I don't have anything to think about except thoughts. So to have something to think about, you must stop thinking some of the time. Just as you must stop talking some of the time to hear what people have to

say. So meditation is the art of stopping thinking for the time being. That's the first stage of it. The best way to do it, instead of trying to stop thinking, is to look at your thoughts as meaningless words."

You know that funny feeling you get by taking a word and repeating it over and over again until it means absolutely nothing and you just think of the sound the word makes? This is what Watts is referring to.

"By this way you tease yourself out of thought and you get into the no thought state. Then when you are in the no thoughts state and you are simply observing the world without commentary, you realize that there are no problems in the world, there is no time, likewise there is no eternity, there is no this and there is no that, because this and that are purely verbal creations. When you do this, you will discover that you can go a stage further, that you can go on thinking and fundamentally preserve an attitude of non-thinking.

You can perfectly well think and conduct all sorts of practical business and live a complete human life, but once you've learned the secret, you can go on because you are no longer fooled by your thoughts."

So not only is meditation a good way to take a step back from the world, it's actually one of the only ways to begin living life with this new attitude. This attitude of non-thinking he is referring to is the same attitude I have referenced throughout the book. It's the attitude of a limitless human being. When we begin meditating on a regular basis, and when we begin to realize the extraordinary benefits that come with it, the whole process of meditation and mindfulness really becomes a lifestyle. Eventually the peace you find in meditation will be the peace you bring to everything you do. Being self-aware and being conscious of thoughts and feelings becomes simple, habitual, and necessary.

Meditation is simply a way to strengthen the mind. Like going to the gym, when we meditate, our mind becomes more efficient, healthy, and useful. On the Netflix series Explained, there were some studies brought up that showed some benefits of meditation. For example, expert meditators have a higher tolerance for pain. There was a test done where meditators and non-meditators were subjected to a painful heat sensation and an MRI scanner was used to measure brain activity.

When most of us anticipate getting burned, our brain's pain center acts as if we were already suffering, and this reaction is so strong when the pain actually arrives, nothing really changes. When that pain is over, mental anguish slowly subsided. Expert meditators react much less in anticipation then they feel the pain very intensely and then activity falls much faster.

Expert meditators, like all of us, can't fully control what happens in their lives but they have much better control over how they respond, and that can be a powerful tool when tensions are high.

This study is a great example of what meditation can do for us if we practice frequently. If an event arises where most people will react with fear, anxiety, worry, or any other kind of negative reaction, the expert meditator would be able to see the situation more clearly and respond in a more solution-oriented way, which can move us forward in life more quickly. Often, if somebody has a "negative" event in life, it can take hours, days, weeks, months, or even years to overcome the event and move forward. Meditators can more easily move past unpleasant events because of this ability to focus and concentrate on the good in life, and the present moment. This is but another fundamental step in our evolution.

Beginning meditation and getting into the present moment is not too difficult and becomes easier over time. It's best to practice with eyes closed and no distractions, but it can definitely be practiced in any environment under any circumstances. Focusing on our breath and our heartbeat is one of the best ways to align with the present moment and with the universe. Our heart and breath are constants, even when we are not aware of them. Becoming aware of that breath and heartbeat brings our awareness to our body in the present moment. The idea here is not to control the breath but to just observe it. Become aware of breaths in and breaths out. While focusing awareness on the breath and heartbeat, all we have to do is listen. Naturally we will lose focus and be distracted by sounds in our environment or thoughts that come to us, but all we have to do is return our awareness to our breath whenever we catch ourselves wondering off. Go with the flow, and find a way back. It's also common to get angry or frustrated if our mind wanders off. A great way to deal with this is to simply acknowledge the wandering as a part of nature that is happening and accept and release the thoughts as they pass through. It's important to know that there are no such things as good or bad thoughts; all thoughts are a part of nature, and like the weather, the thoughts will pass and change. However, they are neither good nor bad. Our perspective makes it so.

Concentration and focus are the main factors that will allow us to return to the present moment and determine whether or not something grows in our lives. If we cannot focus or concentrate, it is extremely difficult to gain momentum in the direction of our desires. Thus, the goal with meditation is to practice concentration. The more we practice, the better we will become. Most people have a tendency to practice distraction in their day-to-day lives, jumping from one topic to the next, from one activity to another, from a conversation with one person to the next, from one social media app to another. Because of all this practice, we are masters at distraction, so it's a matter of breaking this habit and conquering concentration and focus.

There are many other meditations we can practice, and the goal with this particular type of meditation is simply to focus on anything happening in the present moment. It doesn't have to be the breath or the heartbeat. If there is a fan making a consistent white noise, use it. Outside in nature there may be a sound of ocean waves, rain falling, wind blowing in the trees, or a river/stream. By practicing this focus of our awareness, we actually become better at focusing in general and recognizing thoughts or feelings that are passing through us – a great skill to have for many obvious reasons.

If you're looking for something simple and beneficial to focus on, appreciation or gratitude are some of the easiest vibrations to find because many of us live in an environment where we always have clothes, food, water, technology, and many other great blessings. Every new day is actually something to be grateful for because it gives us the opportunity to go out and live our lives. The bottom line is, there are so many things to be grateful for at any moment. The more we practice this vibration, the easier it will be to find.

Eventually, as we practice being in the present moment more and more, we will find that there is a certain distinct feeling that results from this. The more we practice, the more familiar we become with the feeling and the easier it is to access it at any given moment. This feeling can be peace, acceptance, bliss, ecstasy, or any other feeling of pleasure. As we practice meditation, we also begin to realize how much time we spend thinking about the past and the future. It is never wrong to think about the past or the future; there are moments where it may be beneficial and moments where it may not. Finding the balance of thinking about the past, present, and future is a personal preference that can be discovered through this meditation process. I personally recommend a majority of the time be spent in the present moment. The past can be best utilized when it comes to learning a lesson or uncovering information. The future can be used when making plans or setting intentions.

Where can we find the time to do this? If we take a look at how many hours are in a day and see how many discretionary hours we have after doing all of our daily tasks, such as sleeping, eating, working, studying, etc., many people have several hours at their disposal to do whatever they please every day. Take, for example, the average working person who works 40 hours a week. This person sleeps eight hours a day, which is another 56 hours in a week. Let's say their commute to work is 30 minutes there and another 30 back home, so one hour a day, and let's just say that happens seven days a week, so another seven hours. Add the time it takes to prepare meals, use the bathroom, shower, etc. – probably another three hours out of the day each day, so 21 hours a week. That is 124 hours a week spent doing daily tasks but with 168 hours in a week, this would leave the average person with about 44 hours per week of discretionary time to do anything else we choose. That is roughly six hours per day. This is the time that is usually spent watching TV, talking to a friend, reading the newspaper or a book, scrolling through social media, or playing a game. Put simply, we have things in our life that we consider a priority and many of us just need to rethink our priorities. People will make time for things that are important to them. If we really think we don't have time to do a simple exercise that could potentially benefit all areas of our lives, then we need to seriously consider rethinking our priorities and make time for something that will benefit ourselves and the world around us. We all have sacrifices to make and time is definitely one thing that must be sacrificed in the creative process.

An anonymous wise yogi once said "if you don't have time for 20 minutes of meditation, then you need two hours!"

When I first started on my personal development journey, I omitted things like social media, video games, and television. When I did that, I had so much time that I didn't know what to do with it. Cutting out these "priorities" opened my eyes and made me realize just how much time had been spent on these things throughout the years. Honestly I think that taking the time to rethink priorities made a huge positive impact on my life. It is still something I have to do regularly if I catch myself getting off track from my desires, but it is absolutely worth it every single time.

Once we really find the time and begin to practice aligning with the present moment, we can begin to realize some amazing things about the mind and about the universe. The breath especially helps us to learn about both because on one end, we are doing it, and on the other end, it's happening to us. We are breathing and can manage our breath, but at the same time, our breath is automatically taking care of itself – we cannot fully control it. We can see a similar idea when looking at how all creation happens in our lives. On one end, we as humans are doing it, we are creating, and we are making things happen. On the other end, some things are happening to us naturally and we have no control over them. The idea is to find a way to work with nature instead of against it. Find the balance in the work you should do, and the work you should leave to the universe.

Naturally, as humans, we may feel like we are humans experiencing the universe as a separate part of us. The truth is, we are the universe observing and experiencing itself through a human perspective. Sometimes we may observe ourselves when we get angry or upset or anxious, we may do something that we wouldn't normally do, and we may fall back into bad habits – but all of these things are just human nature. We may be aware of what we are doing but we may not necessarily be able to control everything that is happening to our human body. We do play a huge role in what is happening to us as humans, but for the most part, things are going to happen in nature that we cannot control. If someone could control everything, that person just might be called God.

If you are interested in learning more about the art of meditation, I have found YouTube to be a helpful tool to practice with guided meditations. In guided meditations, there is a person instructing you and helping you direct your focus to different areas of the mind and body. These types of meditations are amazing for beginners because they help you get an understanding of what it should feel like to meditate. There are also many meditation apps available to download that may be helpful, such as Insight Timer, Calm, or Headspace. These are great, but they do require a subscription to access most of the content. Personally, I prefer my own free meditation by myself but if you are having trouble, I would definitely consider trying YouTube for the free guided meditations. Then trying out those apps if you're looking for something more organized and official.

Another simple technique that is used to help raise vibrations is keeping some sort of symbol that represents a higher vibration. That vibration and that symbol is intentionally set by us. An example might be a necklace that represents some positive feeling. Many people have used symbols like a special rock or coin or crystal to keep in their pocket, and every time the symbol is touched, it can automatically bring a person to their set vibration for that symbol or it brings the person to the present moment. Some people use this method unintentionally against themselves. For example, people who are afraid of clowns allow them to be a symbol that represents a negative vibration. If we can find these symbols in our life, we can use our willpower to convert negative into positive energy.

Fear is one of the most common negative vibrations and there are many simple methods to overcoming fears if we haven't already figured out how to do so. Some of you may have beliefs holding you back from being brave when it's time to be brave, but being brave does not mean having no fear. Being brave means we feel fear, and we still make the choice to stand up and take action against our fear. When we face our fears directly and realize that they are just temporary vibrations, then we can begin to dramatically change our lives and go places we have never been, do things we have never done, etc. Our fears are nothing but illusions in disguise as something real. The only way to get over a fear is to face it. We all have our own personal relationship with fear. It is something that will always show up in our lives and we just have to practice finding different ways to deal with it. If we try to avoid it, forget it, or go around it, we allow it to continue to show up in our lives. But when we face fear and overcome it, it becomes weaker and appears less often. If it does appear, we know that we have already overcome it and we can trust ourselves to get over it again without much effort.

I specifically remember when I was a child, no older than eight, I was able to overcome the fear in my own mind, and I'll tell you how. I had several brothers, but we had a pretty big house at the time so I slept in my own room by myself. My room was upstairs, farthest away from the bathroom. At night, there were times when I would wake up and need to use the bathroom but I would be too scared to venture into the dark. Like many young children, I was afraid of the dark. Definitely a rational fear for being a child at that age. Then one day I remember badly needing to use the bathroom, knowing I was going to have to get there and probably going to die on the way. But then I actually stopped, thought and asked myself why I was scared. I remember thinking, it's all in my head. Nothing is going to hurt me. I'm in my own house, it's safe. I use the bathroom all the time and I've never been eaten by a monster. There's nothing to be afraid of, I will be fine, and I will feel so much better once I've used the bathroom and am back in bed. So I went out, still feeling the fear but just realizing and learning in that moment that I was creating the fear. Nothing else. From that point forward, I have almost always been able to overcome fears with ease and it's really because of that one lesson I learned. It is all in your head; fear is just an illusion.

We have the choice and the ability to overcome any fear, regardless of what it may be. Let's take the example of a person who is afraid of dogs. I have seen many grown people well into their 50s and 60s who are fearful of small, innocent dogs and by knowing this little trick, that fear could be completely subsided. The reason why people experience fear when exposed to a certain topic is usually because of an experience or a false belief planted by a parent or some other factor in the past. What it all comes down to is just the way we think when that topic comes up. Let's say a person is young and gets bitten by a dog (a powerful negative experience). Every time after that, whenever a dog is in sight or the sound of a dog becomes apparent, that person allows the habitual survival part of their mind to take over and say, "Warning: this is dangerous". That will continue to happen because it is our body's way of keeping us alive and out of danger. However, our body and our mind do not automatically realize that these instincts may be overridden. That person who is afraid of dogs could practice changing their thinking every time a dog situation occurs. Instead of thinking "danger" and other negative thoughts, that person could switch to thoughts like "Not all dogs are dangerous" or "Some dogs are nice and cute." By practicing this over and over again, we eventually teach ourselves a new way of looking at the same situation, which opens the door to a new reality.

Another example is the time I went skydiving. The most common question I get from other people is "Weren't you scared?" I also hear a lot of people say, "I'd be way too scared to ever do that." This one seemed pretty simple to me. If you're thinking about all of the things that can go wrong, yeah, you're probably going to be scared and may never go through with it. I wasn't thinking about the things that could go wrong; I had already played out in my mind exactly what I thought skydiving would be like for me and it was an exciting and amazing adventure. I was just looking forward to seeing the world from a different perspective and to be honest, I never could have imagined anything like it. The point, however, is that fear is all in your mind and can be overcome – once it is conquered, you can live a pretty extraordinary life.

Without meditation and mindfulness, we may still achieve our goals and we may still get what we desire. With meditation and mindfulness, we may have a much smoother and more enjoyable life and we can potentially reach our goals and desires more quickly because of our positive state of mind and ability to manage our thoughts and feelings and overcome obstacles more effectively.

06:
INTERACTING
WITH **PEOPLE**

We are all created **equal**

I nteracting with people is yet another art or skill that we can all learn and improve upon with practice. No matter where we go while on this earth, no matter what we do for work or for pleasure, we are more than likely to come in contact with other people. Some form of communication or cooperation to get what we want. If it's not required, people can still be a big help so communication is important. Everyone is on their own path and learning and growing at their own pace. It's important to remember that even though we may have more experience or knowledge than another person, it does not mean that any person is more important than another. We are all creators and we all have the energy of the universe inside of us working with and guiding us through our everyday lives. The universal awareness and energy may be more apparent in some people than others but nevertheless, it is surely in every person, even if we can't see it in the moment.

Every time we come in contact with a person, we have an opportunity to learn something. Learning is absolutely necessary for our growth and therefore the people we meet are absolutely necessary and important to our growth. If we all treated each other like the most important person in the world, imagine what things would be like. The world would definitely be a better place and we would all evolve much quicker.

A popular statement you may have heard growing up was "treat people the way you want to be treated". It wasn't until recently when I heard the saying that made more sense; "treat people the way they want to be treated". If we want to create a habit of doing this in our lives, we just have to remember one word when interacting with people to make great progress in our relationships and social interactions: empathy. Empathy is putting ourselves in the other person's shoes and attempting to understand things from a different point of view. We mentioned earlier that everyone has a different perspective and beliefs, and these beliefs tend to reveal themselves as a person is speaking about almost anything. By understanding the other person's point of view, we may be able to relate or provide input to a conversation that could potentially benefit oneself or the other person.

Sympathy is something that many people confuse with empathy. The difference is, sympathy does not have the same effect as empathy. With sympathy, you are feeling bad or feeling sorry for the other person who is expressing their negative emotions to you. With empathy, you're understanding the other person and showing them that you understand, but you're not feeling sorry for them. When you feel sorry for someone, it reaffirms the "poor me" mentality to that person. When you show somebody that you understand, but you don't feel sorry for them, it's easier to move forward and it gives the person a message saying "I know what you are going through, you are strong and I know you will get through it". Empathy brings the conversation to the present moment while sympathy brings the conversation back to the past. In all of my years of customer service, I have never had a person get upset with me for showing empathy rather than sympathy. Even though you could tell some people were fishing for sympathy, I didn't give it to them and they ended up being okay with it.

Along with using empathy when dealing with people, we can also approach people with our vibrations in a loving state. With love, there is acceptance, non-judgment, and peace. Each person has a right to their own beliefs and opinions and although we may not agree with other people all the time, we can still accept people the way they are. After all, if everyone were exactly the same and had the same beliefs and opinions, the world would be a very dull place. We need people with opposing opinions for us to more fully solidify our own.

I had the opportunity to be mentored and worked closely with a self-made millionaire for several months. Working with them, I learned a very valuable lesson: Check the fruit on the tree. Many of us may run into a situation where we are doubted or judged, and typically it's only happening because of a lack of vision or understanding. On this path of creation we may also find people giving advice in an attempt to help us or protect us. Be cautious, as this advice may not always be as helpful as it seems to be. This is where the lesson comes into play. When getting advice from someone, see where the information is coming from. Check to see if it's merely opinions or facts that are being given to us. Be aware of what kind of proof or experience the person has. Also, see where that particular advice or beliefs has gotten the person in their lives. For example, if someone is offering relationship advice, but can't keep a healthy relationship to save their life, it's usually a better idea to take advice from someone who has a healthy and happy relationship. If someone is offering financial advice but they can't even pay their own bills on time, it may make more sense to take advice from a person who is financially independent and wealthy. If someone is offering piano lessons but the only instrument they really know how to play is guitar, it's definitely a better choice to take lessons from the person who has been playing the piano since they were young.

This simple idea of checking the fruit on the tree is the most obvious yet one of the most overlooked tips that could potentially make all of our lives better and help us grow much faster. Many people live their lives with beliefs and opinions about the world that were handed down from someone who was attempting to help. What's important to realize is that others' beliefs and opinions are not always helpful and can oftentimes set us back and limit our potential.

From that same mentor, and the people associated with them, I learned the importance of the power of association. They say that you are the average of the five people you're closest with, or the people with whom you spend the most time with. This idea has a similar correlation to conformity. It's important to take a step back and see whom we spend the most time with because the people we are closest with have the biggest influences on our life. For example, if you like to spend time watching football, chances are your closest friends also do. If you smoke cigarettes, chances are your friends smoke as well. If you're a millionaire, chances are that your closest friends may also be financially blessed. When we look at examples like these, we can see clearly that the people we spend time with have a major impact on our lives in many more ways than we think. One important question we can ask ourselves is "Am I living the life I want to live, or am I living the life my friends/family/parents/loved ones want me to live?" Many people live unfulfilled lives because they spend all of their time trying to please other people. Do yourself a favor and think about what you want from a purely selfish point of view, outside of what your peers want. If they really love you, they will accept you and work to understand the changes you decide to make for yourself and in your relationship.

If we want to get ahead of the game, we can make some changes and start spending more time with people who have values or characteristics that you would like to have. Or just spending less time with people who have characteristics and values that you do not want to have. Changing yourself and trying to bring current friends with you usually takes tremendous time, effort, and energy. You can't change people who don't want to be changed. Regardless, all these are great ways to take advantage of the power of association.

If we desire to change our beliefs or habits in a direction that will benefit us, we need to guard our association. This means choosing the people we spend time with wisely. This also means choosing people we talk to or get advice from wisely. For some people, this might mean cutting someone out of our lives completely, changing jobs, or changing living situations entirely. In order to make ourselves and our world a better place, we must make changes, decisions, and sacrifices like this in our lives. It is completely normal to go a separate direction from our friends or family if we think it will benefit our personal development. If we do end up cutting people out, we can always choose to allow people back into our lives once we have developed a strong enough personality and are confident enough to trust ourselves to not be influenced by those people of the past.

Making sacrifices and changes to benefit ourselves, and being honest with the ones we love, may sometimes cause others to be hurt or offended. We all know what it feels like to be offended in some way, shape, or form, and it's not a very pleasant experience. Not to say that it's right or wrong to be offended, but it is something that triggers negative emotions and what most people don't understand is that being offended is a choice. Choices become habits, and many people may have a habit of being offended or annoyed easily. But if we really think about it, being offended has everything to do with our personal perspective. Feeling offended usually comes from a purely selfish point of view. There is an infinite number of ways to view every situation and if we choose to view a situation as something that is offensive or annoying, then it becomes offensive or annoying. Feeling offended stems from the lack of ability to see situations from a non-selfish perspective. Many times when someone feels offended, they think it's because of another person. Oftentimes, that person who is the offender has a point of view that is not meant to be offensive. Even if someone deliberately is trying to offend you, they cannot do so without your permission. So the idea is to look at the situation in a different way, that is, if we desire to no longer feel annoyed or offended.

Along with being offended, there are certain words in every language that is viewed by the average person as "offensive language," which is all based on a purely arbitrary perspective. This also goes back to conformity. Enough people agreed on an idea to the extent that it became the "normal" perspective of most people, even without real reason or truth backing it up. Some people use offensive language in their everyday vocabulary and see it as a way of expressing ideas and opinions, like any other words. Other people may see it as words that are never to be used unless extremely frustrated and out of control. Again, with the infinite possibilities of perspectives, offensive language really is only offensive if we believe it to be. A good example is an innocent child who has no intention of doing harm with words may hear an offensive word and repeat it naturally. After being reprimanded and reprogrammed by a parent or authoritative figure, the child may ask, "Why are bad words bad?" and the real answer that a child will typically never hear is, the words are neither good nor bad. The words are what we make them out to be; it just depends on how we want to look at them.

Another thing to keep in mind when having conversations with people is that some things are better to keep to ourselves. My parents taught me that if you don't have anything nice to say, don't say anything at all. Some people have the tendency to say way more than what needs to be said and by doing this, we can create unnecessary resistance in our lives. So think before you speak, and choose your words wisely.

Along with things we should keep to ourselves, there is something that we should almost never keep to ourselves: our goals and ambitions. There are many people who find success in working in silence and letting their accomplishments do the talking, which is a great way to avoid criticism and hate. What I have learned is that regardless of whether or not we are talking about our goals, there are hateful people in the world and there are people who will always find a way to criticize no matter what. When we speak about our goals and ambitions, they can become more powerful. When we bring up our goals or plans to someone else, there are two basic responses we will find: people who genuinely believe in you and want to see you succeed and will support you, and the opposite. Trust me, if someone believes in you, it will be easy to tell. If someone doesn't believe in you, it's just as easy.

Many people never achieve their goals because they go after them half-heartedly. The way you approach your goals says a lot about you. Many of us are insecure, or we lack confidence in our ability to achieve our goals for whatever reason. The ones who really go out and achieve their goals are the ones who are passionate about their goals. You can usually tell these people are passionate about their goals because they are always talking about and focused on them. The more people we tell about our goals, the quicker we can find people who support us. Genuine support will make goals and desires manifest faster because there's an extra person putting their energy into the dream. Speaking our goals into existence is also good because we can find those people who don't support you and don't believe in you. From that point, we can either cut those people out of our lives completely, or decrease the amount of time and energy spent with them to avoid being dragged down and away from your desires.

If we really want to cut something out of our lives that will save us countless hours of stress, we can start with cutting out arguing. Arguing ruins relationships and can oftentimes ruin our own self confidence. Most arguments happen because of different perspectives or contrasting beliefs about the same topic or situation. Each person believes they are right, and in their mind, they really are. Each of their reasonings are valid to them. Even if the other person is completely wrong, it tends not to be the best idea to point that out to them. Let them figure it out on their own. If someone is wrong and they don't want to believe you, just end the conversation because it can and usually escalate into an argument. The only thing that comes out of an argument is resistance, resistance, and more resistance. The more we argue for our side of things, the deeper we force the other person to dig deeper into their beliefs. The deeper they dig, the more likely that belief is to take hold because they are just finding more and more reasons to be right. The best way to win an argument is to avoid it altogether. Plus, what do we even get out of winning an argument? There is no true prize for winning an argument other than peace, and we can have peace by not arguing at all.

Perhaps the most important thing we can do to improve any relationship or conversation is to listen. The whole point of speaking is to be heard and understood, and to communicate a message that is important. Many people in a conversation get into the habit of thinking about what to say next while the other person is still talking, which detracts focus from what the other person is actually saying. This can often lead to miscommunication, and may often give off a message that one's thoughts are more important than another's. If we really want people to understand and listen to us, we must first learn to understand and listen to others. There is an old saying: "Speak once, listen twice." The more we listen, the more we learn. If we are speaking more than we are listening, we likely are not learning as much as we could be. Every conversation is an opportunity to learn something about that person or about anything in general. If we continue to miss these tiny lessons in conversations, it can have a serious negative impact on our personal evolution over time.

If we really want to take a step in the right direction when it comes to dealing with people, we can stop being "nice" and start being authentic. Being nice is sometimes fake, while being authentic is being real and honest. In most cases, when we are being nice, it's all a front, an act, and an attempt to try and gain respect or approval of another person. Being nice is a way to make other people feel comfortable or welcome, or maybe it's just an egotistical urge to make ourselves look like a good person. Regardless of why we are being nice, by doing so, we often suppress our true thoughts and feelings. Our true thoughts and feelings are really what should be expressed in most conversations if we are to move forward in our evolution as a species. If there is one thing I've learned from years of working and dealing with people, it's that **no matter how nice and polite we are, there are some people who will get upset no matter what**. We are more likely to have someone get upset for being honest or authentic, but this way has a much better chance of bringing the other person into awakening and helping them learn a valuable life lesson. This does not mean going around spewing our opinions; that can get us in trouble. This does mean telling the truth about how you are feeling and what you are thinking. Sometimes the truth hurts – but the truth is the only thing that can set us free, and being authentic and genuine is the best way to set ourselves and people free.

By being authentic and genuine, we can quickly realize where our mistakes are in our belief system or in our attitude. Based on the way people respond to your authenticity, you can learn about yourself and the universe more efficiently than if you were to hide your thoughts, feelings, and beliefs. You also learn a lot about the other person who's responding to your authenticity. Not only do we get more comfortable being authentic and honest with others as we go on, but we also become more authentic and honest with ourselves by doing this. The more honest we are with ourselves, the more likely we are to continue changing in the right direction. If we fail to be authentic and honest with ourselves and others, then we hold ourselves back from realizing many important lessons about the world. Further, we preclude ourselves from teaching other people lessons that they may need to learn for their own personal development. In other words, it's selfish not to be authentic.

One of the most important lessons I have learned by studying multiple successful people in many different areas of life is that helping others and providing value to people has some of the greatest rewards on earth. Of course we should take the time to think about and help ourselves, but we should strike a balance of that with helping other people. The people who have the largest impact and the people who provide the most value are the ones who receive the greatest rewards in life. If we look at this on a level of energy, it's people giving away or sacrificing their own energy and giving it to someone else. The rewards from helping people will not always be given back directly from the people we help, but the universe will find ways to bring that energy back to us – and when it does, it's beyond amazing.

Personally I try to help as many people as I can on a daily basis. When you truly help someone and are able to see the significant positive impact that it has on that person's life, it really does create one of the best feelings in the world, in my opinion. When an old friend of mine was talking to me about their high school track career, they mentioned that they were not good enough to go to state and thus had basically hung up the season. I helped them realize that anyone can go to state and the people who actually end up doing so are not just naturally the best; they just practice and train harder than anyone else. I showed them that by accepting the loss, they are eliminating their potential to become better at the sport. I showed them that by focusing on improving and by believing in themselves, they could potentially still make it to State. I helped my friend zero in on their potential and they were able to come back later and tell me that they took my advice and made it to State. The feeling that you get when someone is genuinely thanking you for something like this is absolutely priceless. Aside from that feeling, rewards from the universe will jump out and surprise you as a result of genuinely helping someone change their life and providing value.

If we take all of the communication techniques we have and condense everything down, we learn to respect other people, let other people talk, use empathy to gain a better understanding, and be honest with other people and with ourselves. Do whatever you can to provide value to other people and receive rewards beyond your imagination. If we can make these tiny shifts in our communication techniques, we are extremely likely to benefit from it in many ways, and the same goes for the other people involved.

07: **DREAMS**

Either you **master your dreams,** or your dreams master you

Dreams are one of the most amazing phenomena that we get to experience as humans, yet they are one of the most overlooked topics of thought and conversation in average everyday life. Some dreams may seem outrageous or irrelevant while others stand out and really make us think about what's going on in our head at night or during the day. There is something to be learned in every experience, and something to be learned from every dream we have. Regardless of how abstract the lesson may appear, we can still learn something about ourselves or the universe from our dreams if we are paying attention.

When we lie down at night to fall asleep, our brain waves begin to change and go through various different cycles. This means that our overall vibration is also changing. Every night when we go to sleep, all of the resistance that we have built up during the day vanishes and a vibration of peace and relaxation typically settles in. Our minds need a break from resistance and action, so sleeping is one of the main ways we obtain this rest. Similarly, meditations are also a way to release resistance, raise our vibration, and give our mind the rest it requires.

Just like normal life experience, dreams contain hidden lessons and if we are able to pay close enough attention, we might actually learn something to apply into our daily lives. Our dreams are glances at our subconscious mind. The subconscious is the part of our mind that controls our breathing, keeps our heart beating, digests food, blinks, swallows, and helps us perform many other everyday tasks with more ease and efficiency, including much of our thoughts, emotions, actions/reactions, and all of our habits. Understanding and relating the subconscious and our dreams to everyday life can help us overcome fears, clear learning gaps, give us ideas and insights of what actions to take to move us closer to our desires in the real world, and sometimes even give us an opportunity to experience our goals being achieved before we actually experience them in real life – like a sneak peek into our future. Being able to correlate dreams to real life can also help us become more clear on our own desires, which is a huge benefit because the sooner we decide and know what we really want, the closer we are to getting it.

Many people are not aware that the average person has several dreams every night. If we have so many dreams, why can't we remember them? The answer is simple. We do not usually remember our dreams unless we set intentions to remember them. Most of the time when we remember dreams, we do so unintentionally, or we may remember a dream because of a very intense feeling that was experienced within the dream. Our brain has an amazing function that records experiences that contain extreme emotions, and helps us remember when things made us feel really bad or really good. This is why most of our vivid memories of the past are usually those of extreme pain or pleasure. Although this is a great way we can use our memory, this is not the only way we remember important experiences or information. Setting intentions not only helps us take action when action is required, but it's a great way to remember anything we want to remember. When studying for a test, we tend to approach the process with the intention to remember the information we are studying. When we go into any kind of relationship, we set intentions to remember certain things about the other person. If we want to remember our dreams and begin reaping the benefits, we must first set intentions to remember our dreams.

Another reason why we may not remember our dreams is because we have limiting beliefs that block us from being able to remember. Limiting beliefs might be something as simple as "I can never remember my dreams." Just because something has not been done in the past does not mean we cannot do it in the present moment or in a future moment. If we continue to say to ourselves and others "I can never remember my dreams," we will continue living that reality. Setting intentions for dreams is the most simple and effective way to remove negative blocks and begin to remember our dreams. The best way to do this is to start recording or writing down our dreams. Most people have a morning routine when waking up and there tends to be something close by that we grab as soon as we find the energy to get out of bed. For most people, this may be a cellphone, alarm clock, or maybe a glass of water. Right before going to bed, place a notebook and pen near your bed and label the top of the paper "Dreams" or something similar. Taking this action right before going to sleep sets the intention of remembering our dreams, and waking up with the visual reminder of the notebook helps us to remember we set the intention. By doing this, we should be able to find success pretty seamlessly. If you are somebody who wants to start remembering dreams, I highly recommend repeating this step until you can remember at least one part of a dream each night for a full week.

The goal is to remember as many of our dreams as we can and record as much detail as possible for each dream. After a while, we will find ourselves remembering multiple full dreams each night. By doing this consistently, we program our mind to recall our dreams subconsciously with much less effort and we can begin to dissect our dreams each morning to learn something new about ourselves or the world around us. Recording and remembering dreams also increases our ability to tell the difference between dreams and reality. The more we are able to distinguish dreams from reality, the more likely we are to have what is known as a *lucid dream.*

Lucid dreaming can be an extremely beneficial gift for those who have recurring nightmares or for anyone who wishes to explore the universe through the dream world and take full or partial control of their dreams. The only thing that differentiates lucid dreaming from a normal dream is that we become aware that we are in a dream while we are in it, and at that point, if we realize and understand that dreams can be manipulated with our mind, we can begin to explore, change, create, or become anything within the dream. During any dream, anything is possible. The choice is yours to decide what happens in front of you during a lucid dream, and it is completely up to your ability to imagine. If you would rather just be lucid in a dream and let the environment do its own thing, that's another option you have. Lucid dreaming is a skill like any other and can be learned and developed over time.

It will take time and patience in order to have your first lucid dream. Lucid dreaming is not something that can be forced; just as with many things, it must be allowed and happen naturally but we must first put in the work and begin to set intentions for our dreams. The best way to prepare for a lucid dream is to close your eyes and *imagine* what it would be like to be in a dream where you have full control of your motor functions and full feeling in your body. Imagine being able to wiggle your toes and move your fingers and feel the sensation happen as if it's real. Now imagine any kind of scene you desire and think of all the specific details – what it would look like, smell like, feel like, and so on. Based on my own experience and those of others, if you are not visualizing what you want to dream about, it is much more difficult and you are less likely to find yourself in a lucid dream. It's not impossible, but your chances are much higher if you know exactly what you want to dream about or what you desire to create within the dream.

After several years of experience with lucid dreaming, I began to discover there were many methods to begin lucid dreaming. Every source I've learned from recommends that we should start out by remembering dreams in general. One of the main methods that I see is called the Wake Back to Bed method, or WBTB. It requires you to set an alarm for approximately 4.5 hours into your sleep cycle to wake you up, and then fall back asleep. The reason for 4.5 hours is because for most people, your mind will be in the REM cycle during this time, which is where most dreams tend to occur, thereby making it much more likely that you wake up from a dream and/or fall asleep going right into a dream. What I've done personally when using this method is fall back to sleep while replaying the last dream I can remember in my head over and over. Whether that dream was just before I woke up or weeks ago, I just remember every detail possible. If everything goes as planned, you should pop right back into that same dream or another, and you may become lucid.

Another method to try that has worked for me is the falling method. Imagine the feeling of falling as detailed as possible. If you've never jumped off cliffs or been skydiving, you might be able to imagine jumping on a trampoline and falling that way. As long as you can imagine yourself being pulled down toward the earth, feel the gravity, and the falling sensation, then you are doing it right. If this method works out, you will enter into your lucid dream by falling right out of the sky or you may feel like you're tumbling out of your bed, but you're really just falling in the dream, and from that point it's game on.

Another simple technique that many people seem to be teaching is to go throughout the day questioning reality. This means looking at things around you and asking yourself, "Am I dreaming?" The more you ask that question while you're awake, the more likely you are to subconsciously ask yourself that question while you're asleep, and the more likely you are to have a lucid dream.

If you are someone who absolutely cannot seem to make lucid dreams happen with any method, you might consider trying lucid dreaming pills. Personally, I've discovered that these pills work for me, but I didn't discover these until years after I had been lucid dreaming and decided to try them for fun. I would recommend researching drug facts and side effects of a pill called LucidEsc, made by the company called ViviDream. This pill is designed to assist with dream recall and awareness, which are the skills required to lucid dream. I would only recommend this method as a last resort. The last thing you want is to create a false belief that "I can only lucid dream if I take this pill." I want to help people create a real lucid dreaming career, not just a one-time lucid dreaming experience, and definitely not a full-time, pill-popping lucid dreaming career.

When we finally have our first lucid dream, it may be alarming and we may get so excited that it actually wakes us up and ends the dream. There are multiple different ways for a lucid dream to start out. It can begin out of nowhere all of a sudden, or it can happen right in the middle of a non-lucid dream. Whenever we find ourselves becoming aware that we are in a dream, the key is to just stay calm, relax, and enjoy the experience. While dreaming, it's important to keep these things in mind: You can't actually die in a dream, fear is an illusion, and anything is possible. You are 100% safe and will not be harmed in any way. If we can keep these ideas in mind, we can do anything we want in our dreams. Earlier in the book we talked about facing fears directly. I personally have had normal dreams and lucid dreams where my fear was running straight at me full speed. I would feel the fear and brace for impact but then I would remember that it's only an illusion and it can't hurt me. From that point, I was able to look my fear straight in the eyes as it jumped toward me to attack me, but right as it hit me, it vanished because I was able to stand my ground and trust that I would be okay. This is possible for anyone; it may be easier said than done, but with practice we can master this ability.

The more we understand lucid dreams, the more we will realize some pretty amazing truths about ourselves and the way our mind works. With these truths, we can not only apply them to our dreams, but also to our everyday lives. Here are just a few things I have realized through my own lucid dreaming experiences.

- We can't create what we want until we have imagined and visualized it first. The only manifestations I have been able to successfully create during a lucid dream are ones I have visualized while awake. When attempting to create something I have not visualized, the manifestation fails or turns into something similar but not exactly what I was intending. Regardless, the best way to create is to visualize a few minutes every day. Typically this works best right before falling asleep or as soon as we wake up. The best manifestations come out of the ideas we visualize most. The most clear lucid dream I have ever created was a scene where I was on the beach with my toes in the sand, the warm sun beating down on my skin, with the sound and sight of the ocean, and palm trees all around. This was something easy for me to create in the dream because I had replayed the image in my mind every day for several weeks. This also is the same for life outside of dreams. When attempting to create something in your life, visualization helps so much with the process and makes things happen more smoothly.

- Using effort or "trying" does not help with the creation process but actually hinders it. When I first started lucid dreaming, the first thing I wanted to experience was flying like a superhero. I was surprised to find out that it actually took practice; it took me about four flying lucid dreams before I finally got it down to a point where I could travel freely and explore. The biggest problem I had was that I tried really hard to force myself into the air and make the environment cooperate with me and I soon realized that the more I strained myself and "tried," the more I would fail by falling to the ground or just waking up. The more I practiced, the less I felt like I had to put in effort and the easier it became. This is the same in real life. When you are forcing or trying too hard to make something happen, you create resistance. The key is to trust and go with the flow.

- Our manifestations may not turn out exactly the way we want them, especially on the first try. I went through a stage of lucid dreaming when I was really into cars and was practicing visualizing driving many of my favorites, one being a Rolls Royce. I attempted to create my first-ever Rolls Royce during a lucid dream and it was beautiful, except for when I got inside. It was very cartoonish or looked like an underdeveloped videogame. Nevertheless, I had created my dream car and was able to experience the incredible feeling of a v12 engine pushing me against my seat as I accelerated. The next few cars I created in my dreams were much more realistic; they just took some fine tuning. Regardless of how our creations end up, we can still find ways to appreciate them and enjoy them. This again is the same when it comes to real life and it's pretty self-explanatory. We won't always get exactly what we want when creating something in real life, but we can still appreciate the things we do create and learn from each creation.

- Although we are creators, we don't create everything; we are co-creating with the rest of the universe. My first two or three years of lucid dreaming consisted of focusing on creating specific objects or experiences, which was great, but eventually I realized that I had never had a lucid dream where I just wandered around and experienced the creations that were happening naturally in the dream world. This is when my lucid dreams became the most exciting because there were many surprises and challenges and I was still able to create something if I had the desire. In real life, it's the same way. We are co-creating with the universe and we are never in full control of what's going on in our lives.

Dreams are really just like another reality, like the real world, with laws and rules. Some rules are similar and some different, and understanding dreams can help us better understand reality by comparing and contrasting. One of the biggest differences between dreams and reality is that in dreams, creation is instantaneous, whereas in reality, creation takes time. There is still the same concept of our thoughts and perspective creating and changing the environment, except for our dreams reflect energy back to us immediately. Our dreams are just a way of showing us the result of our thoughts and perspectives minus the time delay we experience in reality. Our thoughts and perspectives in reality are still immediately causing the environment to change but it happens so subtly and unexpectedly that we often don't notice until some drastic change occurs in our environment. In dreams, we have all the same creative abilities, except they are magnified and greatly exaggerated. It's so important to understand that we have the same creative potential in reality; we just have to have patience and work with the rules that the universe has in place.

Dreams are important, whether you've ever found a use for them or not. Take my advice when I say that dreaming can completely change your life. For me personally, it is almost like having two separate realities. Being able to lucid dream and remember my dreams regularly makes me excited to go to sleep each night and hop into the dream world, and after spending much time in the dream world, I'm just as excited to wake up and go experience the real world each morning.

08: APPLYING
KNOWLEDGE

Effort is required to create
what you desire

N ow comes the part where we face reality. Obviously it would be amazing if all we had to do is change our minds to attract what we desire, but this is really just the first step of many. Everything we create must first exist as a thought before it can exist in reality, and our thoughts are followed by our words and actions. If we really want to get leverage on our lives and create a more desirable present moment and future, one of the best things to do is reflect on our daily actions and habits. Recognize and replace old habits with new habits that serve you better. Creating new habits can be as easy or as difficult as we make it. Creating a new habit usually does not happen without abandoning an old one. We have to sacrifice the good for the great.

When we create a beneficial habit for ourselves, we basically put ourselves on auto-pilot toward our desires. You may be asking, how does someone create a beneficial habit? There are many ways to create a beneficial habit but first it's important to understand the habit itself. When we really go into understanding a habit and what it actually is, we can better manage ourselves and our habits.

In the 1989 book *The Seven Habits of Highly Effective People,* author Stephen Covey says, "Our character, basically, is a composite of our habits. 'Sow a thought, reap an action; sow an action, reap a habit; sow a habit, reap a character; sow a character, reap a destiny,' the maxim goes.

Habits are powerful factors in our lives. Because they are consistent, often unconscious patterns, they constantly, daily, express our character and produce our effectiveness...or ineffectiveness."

A brilliant entrepreneur and author named James Clear did an amazing job of describing habits. I ran into his work on YouTube, but he has also written books and does public speaking. In the video that I watched, he said, "It's actually the anticipation or hope or prediction of what is to come that motivates all action." This is true on many levels. Clear breaks down habits into four laws; cue, craving, response, and reward. The reason why any action takes place is because of some sort of cue, whether that be a thought or a smell or something we see or maybe a sound. The cue could be anything. That cue then turns into a craving or a desire. From that desire, we create some sort of response. From our response, we get some sort of reward. We can use these four stages of habit to break old undesirable habits and create ones that will assist us in creating a more desirable life. Some people may feel like their habits are in control, but after some learning and practice, you will realize that you are in control of your habits.

When starting a new habit, we can use the four laws of habit to help us stay on track. With cue, the idea is to make the cue obvious. This could be writing a sticky note and putting it on the mirror in the bathroom. Next is craving. The idea here is to make it attractive. Making it attractive could be thinking of all the benefits that might come out of it. Then response: make it easy. If we think something will be difficult, we generally won't do it, so making it seem as simple as possible is a great idea. For the reward, this could be anything that makes us feel good and proud about what we have accomplished. Psychologically, we can call this positive reinforcement and it is used with humans and animals to create or break habits. On the flip side is negative reinforcement, which uses fear or pain or negative rewards as punishment.

To break bad habits, we can use the same four laws of habit. For cue, the idea is to make it invisible. If the goal is to stop watching so much television, put the TV in another area of the house where it won't be used as much, or flip the couch around so it's not facing the television. For craving, make it unattractive. If the goal is to stop smoking, watch videos about the smokers who lose their voice or look up pictures of smokers' lungs. For response, make it difficult. If the goal is to play less video games, put the games away in a hard-to-reach place that would take a lot of work to get out and set up. For reward, make it unsatisfying. This would be something like making yourself clean the bathroom or do some kind of chore after choosing to eat a whole bag of potato chips in one sitting, as a punishment. Breaking a bad habit could also be as simple as retelling the story for what each que means or what kind of reward you would get out of it. An example of that could be like instead of seeing a pack of cigarettes and thinking "I'm going to smoke", think "I'm gonna eat an apple". It could literally be anything, as long as the cue is changed to make you do something more beneficial than the bad habit.

Clear says that our daily actions are like a vote for the type of person we want to become. If we look at the things we are doing on a daily basis, and if we continue on the same path for two, five, or 10 years, imagine what kind of impact our habits will have on our lives. So whether they're good or bad habits, our character depends on what we do daily, so choose wisely.

If we really think about it, we will realize that we can become any kind of person we want to become and we can do anything we want to do in our lives on this earth. Musical artist Big Sean has a great saying that holds a lot of truth. He says in his song *Who's Stopping Me,* "I pray that you got the courage to flourish, on all your urges, whether it's a new dream or refurbished, understand, nothing off limits if it's on this earth b**** so let's get to work." We all have to start somewhere and we all have to end somewhere. What we do in that time is up to us.

When it comes to figuring out what we want in life or figuring out what we should do next, an easy place to start is to take out an old-fashioned pen and paper, and write down a few things. Making a list of qualities we would like to have as a person is going to immediately set us in the right direction. Then make a list of experiences we would like to have in our lifetime, as well as a list of any other goals or plans we might have for the future, places we want to go, people we want to meet, things we want to see or accomplish. These plans and goals should be short-term and long-term. Short term meaning things we can change today, this week or this month.

Long term meaning things we want to see manifested further down the road. Make this list as detailed and specific as possible while writing down any and all ideas. These lists can be updated and changed later on if desired. Personally I recommend a full update on this list at least once a year. New Year's is a good time to make that move. Once this list has been created, we can get a very good idea of what kind of life we will end up having in the future if we choose to start putting in the work in the present moment.

> *"If you don't make plans for yourself you'll probably always fit into someone else's plans. Guess what someone else might have planned for you?*
> *Not much!" - Jim Rohn*

After you've created your own list, the next best thing to do is to ask yourself why. Why do I want the things I want? What would be true about my life if we were able to manifest all of my desires? How would I feel when my desires are finally manifested into physical reality? After all of those questions have been asked, ask yourself; do I really want to put in the effort to create this? The goal here is to really feel and experience (vibrationally) what it would be like to live the life you desire. It was mentioned earlier that when you mix thought and emotion together, you create that coherence that is required to fuel your actions toward your desires. So when doing this, you want to bring yourself to feel real joy, excitement, love, surprise, etc. If you're having a hard time imagining how it would feel to experience these events that haven't happened yet, try imagining events that you have already experienced in the past and use those feelings to find similar feelings in the future. Think of the happiest past experiences you've had and use them as fuel to bring you to the future. It's very important to remember that all we are doing here is setting our preferences for what we would like to experience vibrationally. Everything that we desire in life all comes down to wanting pleasant vibrations within and around us. Once we realize this, we can start on the next logical step, which is figuring out how to get what we desire. As mentioned earlier, we don't always get what we want, but we do get what we deserve. To achieve success in anything, we must first earn it. There is no way the universe will allow someone to achieve success if they don't truly deserve it or take the necessary steps to earn that success.

Another vitally important step we should take in this process is to ask ourselves what kind of sacrifices need to be made if we want to reach our goals. We also need to ask ourselves if we are willing to make those sacrifices and commit once we say yes. For example, if one of your goals is to become more physically fit, you may have to sacrifice eating potato chips or going to fast-food restaurants. If you want to start your own business, you may have to sacrifice watching TV or perusing social media to give yourself more time to do research and plan for your success.

Once we have our goals set, we need a plan. Antoine de Saint-Exupéry said, "A goal without a plan is just a wish." Warren Buffett, one of the wealthiest men in the world, said, "An idiot with a plan can beat a genius without a plan." If you can't think of a plan right away, do some research and see what other people are doing to achieve goals similar to yours. There are multiple different routes we can all take that will lead us to our desires and we just need to find and choose one of them to stick with. If you can't seem to bring yourself to a plan, be patient, a plan will reveal itself to you. If you're waiting for a plan, it may be because you haven't formed solid goals yet. If you're in that position, go back and work on your list of goals again, making them even more specific and diving deeper into the reason why you want to manifest those goals. Once you have formulated solid goals and a solid plan, start putting in the work immediately. Be ready and willing to make mistakes because I guarantee they will happen; they are also what will make you grow and turn you into a better person.

It's important to understand that making plans does not always mean that things will go exactly as planned. In fact, you should expect to reach a point where an improvised plan will be required. Expect the unexpected. There is an anonymous quote that goes "if the plan doesn't work, change the plan but never the goal." It could be easy to become discouraged if things don't work out the way we want them to, but we must remember that everything happens for a reason, and everything happens at the perfect moment, when we are vibrationally ready. We will eventually realize that the unexpected plans or changes are some of the most valuable decisions we end up making on this journey, and they contain some of the most valuable lessons as well.

Lil Wayne "Ain't 'bout what you walk away from, it's 'bout what you walk away with"

From that point, we can know and trust that everything we desire on that list will come to fruition in our lives in some way, shape, or form. As long as we are doing our part. Exercise patience. Be grateful for everything that has already been created and for the ability to continue creating – this will raise our vibration to be ready to deserve and receive what we ask for. Go through the day living in the moment as much as possible and watch for the miracles. The more we are waiting and watching, the more we will recognize them. In the Christian Bible, Luke 11:9 says, "Ask, and it will be given to you; seek, and you will find; knock, and it will be opened to you." We can always find what we are looking for, so it might as well be something amazing.

This list of our goals is probably one of the most critical activities we could do when it comes to creating the life of our dreams. The trouble with most people is not with achieving their goals. The problem is usually that people don't set goals at all, and just leave everything to chance or hope. According to Bill Gates, "You have to pick a pretty finite number of things to tell your mind to work on. You have to decide... What should you care about?" And this is very true. I personally use the idea of putting all of your eggs in one basket. Once we have decided what we want in our life, we will notice many potential routes in life opening up that may lead to the life we desire. The idea is not to say yes to every single route that we find. The idea is to pick something, stick with it, and then once that is pretty solid and habitually running itself, you can choose to add more. We can be easily overwhelmed if we try to take on too many tasks at once.

At first, once I started practicing this new mindset and made my own goals, I was taking new opportunities and trying new things left and right. The problem was, I wasn't putting enough time, effort, and energy into one thing long enough to see it work the way I wanted to, so I was disappointed in myself time and time again. When I finally learned about the eggs in a basket rule, I decided on one thing that I could put my time into, jumped on it, cut out almost everything else, and put all of my focus there. This book is where I chose to put my energy and it's now fully published and in your hands because I followed through with the same lessons you are learning now.

Along any journey, there will be trials, challenges, and surprises that seem to appear out of nowhere. There will be times where everything around you seems to be pushing you to give up and quit – this is where most people will fail and revert to their old ways. The Promised Land is available to anyone who can overcome and work through the struggles. These struggles are tests given to us by the universe in an attempt to see if we are truly ready for the things we desire. The key is to keep going and trusting that there will be light at the end of the tunnel even if there are no signs and all hope seems to be lost. All we need is the tiniest bit of faith and effort and as long as we are putting in the work, the universe will respond and the darkness will be lifted when the time is right.

Most of my personal goals could not be achieved in a day's work. While working, I find that it's normal to desire instant gratification, but in most cases that is not the reality we experience. It took months to actually start completing my goals and years for others. If I ever found myself lacking the energy to take action, I would simply remind myself of my goals and know that they would be realized once the required work was done. We must be willing to work until we have built up the patience, persistence, and discipline. If we cannot bring ourselves to trust the process, we will likely stay put until we can learn to work without seeing instant results. Interestingly, I realized through this process that making the goals and achieving them isn't the best part, even though it may seem that way at first. The best part is the journey along the way, the lessons learned, and the person you become through the process. If we decide for ourselves that reaching the goal is the most important part of this process, we will get to a point where the goal is reached, and then we will realize that all of the actions we have been taking and everything that we have been thinking has been for that one moment. This usually causes people to stop working, stop changing, and stop moving forward because it seems like your purpose has been reached, and there's nothing left to do. This personal development journey is one that we take on for life. If you want to become the best version of yourself, you must never stop learning, challenging, and changing yourself.

"No matter how many mistakes you make or how slow you progress, you are still way ahead of everyone who isn't trying"- Tony Robbins

Another thing to keep in mind about our desires is that we can't just write them down, forget about them and expect them to show up, or get upset when they don't show up. Desire is like a plant. When writing down desires and goals, you are essentially planting a seed, which must be tended to and cared for until the point where it is ready for harvest. For some desires, daily action will be required to reach where you want to be. Thus, exerting even the tiniest bit of effort each day or as often as possible is necessary for staying on track with these desires. For those desires which we cannot take daily action, our only duty is to act when the universe prompts us to act. Trust me, you will know when it's time to act on those desires.

Through this process, we will also learn that some desires can manifest almost instantly if we are in the right place at the right time, and if we are asking in the correct way. How do we know if we are in the right place at the right time? Check your vibration. If you're feeling like you are on top of the world and having an amazing time, you're most likely in the right place at the right time. It may be on a hike, on the beach, with friends, or by yourself. Any moment that feels like absolute bliss is usually the best time to ask the universe for something we want to manifest. When our vibration is high and we are thinking of a desire to send to the universe, we have created that unique combination of brain and heart coherence that can move mountains.

One day, I was on a hike with one of my good friends. The hike was a few hours long and filled with appreciation and being in the moment. On the way down a trail, we started talking about how hungry we both were. It also happened to be crabbing season and we were discussing how much we craved some crab. Not even a week later, my friend messaged me out of the blue saying a long-time neighbor had appeared at their front door offering three giant fresh crabs as a gift. This neighbor clearly had not known of our chat on the hike and this was their first encounter in months, maybe years. Yet out of all the things possible, we were able to get our crab delivered to our doorstep without any physical effort, simply because of the way we asked the universe.

I personally have created a straightforward test to teach some new creators about how simple the creative process can be. I have tested this with myself and two other people and all three of us were able to create this manifestation. First, I made sure we were in a peaceful mood and setting to begin with. Then, I started by asking: have you ever found money on the ground? Then: where were you? Whom were you with? What did it feel like? These are all asked with the intent of getting that person to recreate the vibration in their mind of something amazing being manifested. After that, we simply moved on with our day and never brought up the topic again. I told each of them "just wait, soon it will happen again". I hadn't found money on the ground for several years prior to this activity, and within two weeks it happened. No just spare change; actual cash on the ground. My brother was one other person who participated and he found money within a month. My other friend, whom I was teaching, found money on the ground within two or three months.

In order to get what we want, we need to find a way to feel those feelings or that vibration of already having what we want. We may not be able to bridge the gap between where we are and where we want to be if we cannot find this feeling. Ask (think about what you want) when vibrations are already high and try to avoid asking when vibrations are low. Then it is a matter of imagining the way you would feel by already having it. Often, if our vibration is high, we do not have to search far to find the feeling of having our desires manifested. It is more difficult to find the feeling when in a low vibration simply because in those moments we are not thinking good thoughts or feeling good feelings. If you're already thinking and feeling good thoughts and feelings, it's going to be much easier to find others.

As we begin to familiarize ourselves with this advanced way of being, we may notice that we receive impulses of thought or good ideas just appearing out of nowhere. Many people call this intuition. Intuition is usually the first thought that comes to our mind when we are approached with some sort of task or anything where we may be required to take physical action. This is the next piece of work required to move toward our desires. It is common for people to ignore or reject intuition, but we should realize that intuition is our best friend. These are the moments where we have a "gut feeling" or a sudden urge. As we practice working on our relationship with the universe, our intuition will become more and more valuable. The key is to trust that feeling, even if it may not seem right at first. Eventually it will be very easy to recognize an impulse from our intuition. The path of least resistance can almost always be uncovered by listening to our intuition. The only way to reach our desires is to listen and be ready to take action when it's time, so it is very important to maintain this relationship.

"Your intuition always whispers, it never shouts... it's very hard to hear. You have to be ready and listening every day for the rest of your life." -Steven Spielberg

Intuition can also be helpful when it comes to improvising. As mentioned earlier, our plans will not always end up exactly the way we intend, so improvisation comes in quite handy in these situations. If we already have a good relationship with ourselves and our intuition, we can improvise like pros. Sometimes an improvised decision may be one of the most important decisions we make so there's just another reason why that relationship is so important. A good way to connect with our intuition and lead ourselves down the path of least resistance is to flip a coin when making decisions. By doing this, we get a sense of which side we want the coin to land on, whether it happens while the coin is flipping in the air or once the coin has shown heads or tails. If we pay attention, we can figure out what we really want in that moment based on what our intuition tells us, or based on how we feel once the coin has decided. The idea is to go with the path that feels the best in that moment.

> *"Moving to the rhythm of my intuition, anything I want I speak into existence, that's how I'm living, that's how I'm winning" - Russ*

Sometimes these impulses from intuition will be so sudden and random that we might miss or forget the amazing thought flowing through us. An easy way to ensure we retain great ideas is to start taking notes and/or journaling regularly. Many people in the modern age carry a cell phone, and cell phones come equipped with an app just for taking notes. This makes it easy and convenient to quickly jot down any thoughts or good ideas. If taking notes on a phone doesn't sound appealing, write on a sticky note, notepad, or even your hand. You can also just carry a journal with you wherever you go but that may be more of a hassle. In this universe of infinite possibilities, one thought could be a million dollar idea that changes the world. You might use your notes, you might not. The key is to write down as many as possible, just in case.

Melanie Robbins, author of the book *The 5 Second Rule*, has a very accurate way of describing how intuition works, and why it doesn't work for some people. Robbins says that people who are stuck in some kind of bad situation or habit are there because they can't seem to do the right thing, even though they know what the right thing is. The reason why this happens is because our intuition requires action immediately. Mel says it takes about five seconds for us to convince ourselves out of action or a good idea, so the key is to think and act simultaneously to stay on track with our desires. Avoid overthinking, especially when it comes to making decisions. Just choose a path and go with the flow. This is a skill that takes practice and with time, we can master it just like the rest.

Alan Watts, as mentioned earlier, also talks about thinking and acting simultaneously. Watts mentioned a story about a man fighting a bear where the bear could read the man's mind. Every move the man would make, the bear would be one step ahead. The only way the man was able to defeat the bear was to not think about what he was going to do before he did it. In other words, making a move at the exact same time as the thought so that the bear could not possibly predict what was happening next. Watts called this outwitting the devil, saying, "If your plan is to outwit the devil, it might be best not to give him any advance notice that you're about to do so."

When it comes to making decisions, it is common to analyze the situation, variables, and other determining factors to help make our decision. If we really wanted to, we could analyze the situation for eternity because in reality, there are an infinite number of variables and possibilities and we can never fully predict all of them even if we try. The moment we take action is usually when we have run out of time to think and are forced to choose. We can call this time of analyzing and thinking hesitation. When we are working with our intuition and learning to act without hesitating, we may get into trouble every now and then, but we will find that we strengthen our relationship with our intuition and it becomes more useful to us in every moment.

You may be asking yourself, "How do I know when a decision is the right decision to make?" Simply put, you don't. There is no way to tell exactly in every situation if the decision you're making is the right or the wrong decision. Sometimes it may be unclear which decision to choose but in situations like this, all you can do is just send it (Use your best judgment to make a decision, take action, and trust that everything will work out).

Earlier it was recommended to make goals and plans, and write them down. This can also be known as setting intentions, which we talked about as a method to help remember dreams. Setting intentions, outside of our dream life, could be as simple as saying something like "I will have a good day today." By doing this, we set our minds on a mission and are very likely to complete a task if we actually have a set task to fulfill. If we give our mind a task like "Look around the room and find all the things that are blue," our mind will automatically begin finding things that are blue. At the same time, we probably will not notice anything that was green or red simply because our mind was searching exclusively for blue. This works the same way with all intentions and anything receiving our focus. If we are looking for evidence of a good day, we will find it. At the same time, we will usually block out anything else as long as we remember our intention that was set. If we are looking for things to complain about or things to get upset about, we will find them. So, by setting our intentions early in the day, week, month, or year – generally early in life – we are much more likely to be aware of the signs along the way that will help lead us to our desired intention. Even if you missed the opportunity to start early, it is never too late to start setting good intentions.

Making plans and setting intentions for ourselves is a great way to get organized and a great way to build momentum in the right direction. When we neglect to do what's good for us, like making plans or goals, or changing habits, we might make an excuse or say something like "I will do it later." If we put it off, what we are really doing is setting ourselves up for failure. There will always be an excuse if we look for one and the idea is to set a time and a place for things that are important to us. Jim Rohn, as mentioned earlier, is an American entrepreneur, author, and motivational speaker. He has a great philosophy around the idea of neglect worth sharing:

"The things that are easy to do are also easy not to do. That's the difference between success and failure... I did not neglect to do the easy things I could do for X years."

He continues:

"Major reason why you don't get what you want in America, simple answer, neglect. It starts as an infection and if you don't take care of it, it becomes a disease. One neglect leads to another. You could do it, you should do it, you don't do it!? That's called a formula for disaster. All you've gotta do is let that and a couple other things accumulate for X years and now you're driving what you don't want to drive, wearing what you don't want to wear, living where you don't want to live, doing what you don't want to do, maybe having become what you don't really want to become. This stuff is not difficult."

Ask yourself, is there a way I can change this? If the answer is yes, work toward changing it and making it better, but only if you want to. If the answer is no, then accept it the way it is. Don't try to change things that can't be changed. Don't neglect to change things that can and should be changed.

Along with making plans and goals and setting a time and a place for our plans and goals, if we strive to challenge ourselves, we are setting goals in the right direction. When working toward goals, it's important to do more than we thought we could do, and finish what we started. Take someone who wants to get in better shape, who sets a goal to do three sets of 10 pushups each day. An optimal approach to this would be to do something like 11 pushups in each set and finish the entire three sets. By doing so, we show ourselves that our willpower is stronger than we anticipated and we begin to strengthen our confidence and our mindset around that task.

When we are performing some kind of task or trying to accomplish something, it's common to feel the need to rush and get to the end in a hurry. One thing we can remember to help us is to focus on the activity, not the outcome. Slow and steady wins the race. In other words, if we rush and stress to get things done, we can easily miss fine details, leave things undone, or cause other unforeseen problems. Focusing on the present moment is by far the best way to complete any task. The present moment is where our power is. Test this out while completing a simple activity around the house and be amazed with how productive and peaceful that activity can actually be.

Another common area where people misplace their awareness is in comparing progress. Everyone grows at different rates and anyone who is successful in any field was once an amateur, so it doesn't make sense to compare the beginning of our journey to the end of someone else's. Everyone who is a master at anything was once in the shoes of a beginner. All creation takes time so if we are just beginning to create something new in our lives, let it happen naturally and do not try to force it. If we stay in our own lane and focus on our own progress and results, we can make it to where we want to be. Never be discouraged by someone else's manifestations in life. All of our wishes won't come true overnight, but we can trust that they will come true in time if we do our part.

Something else we can practice is being honest with ourselves. We talked about being authentic and honest earlier, but here are a few more helpful ideas. The truth can sometimes hurt and thus is often avoided. If we can be brutally honest with ourselves and dive deep into any place where we find resistance, we can move forward and raise our vibration on any subject. One way to practice honesty is to look ourselves in the eyes (in a mirror) and ask ourselves a question. By doing this, it is easy to tell whether or not we are being honest, and we can work on improving that. When we are honest with ourselves, we strengthen our self-trust and we begin to make better decisions about what is good for us versus what is not. Honesty and truth will help keep us on the path of least resistance.

When it comes to staying on the path of least resistance, we will surely run into opposition along the way. If we didn't, it would be called the path of no resistance. Resistance is what makes us grow, and what doesn't kill you makes you stronger. Much of the resistance we may encounter along the way is going to come from other people in our lives. Think about anyone who has ever created anything amazing on this earth. The person who said, "We're going to land a spaceship on the moon" was probably judged, criticized, and ridiculed many times. The first person to invent the smartphone – a phone without buttons! – was definitely challenged as well. Anything that is considered out of the ordinary will almost always be criticized, judged, or challenged by people who do not understand that anything is possible. This judgement and criticism is not always intentionally to damage or harm anyone, but it usually takes place due to a lack of understanding on how the universe works, so don't take it personally.

In order for humans to evolve, change, and move forward in society, we need people who are willing to think outside of the normal way of thinking. The normal way will continue to create what already exists. A new way of thinking is required to create something that does not yet exist. We cannot solve problems in the same state of mind that is creating the problem. So when it comes to resistance from friends, family members, or any person, we must realize that that person is still trapped in the illusion of the past, while we have evolved. We do not need others' approval to do what is right for us in our own lives. It is completely up to us and we are able to make our own decisions on what we want to create in our lives and how we want to live.

Jim Rohn had a very powerful statement about change:

"If you will change, everything will change for you. You don't have to change the government, you don't have to change prices, you don't have to change taxes, forget all that. And the first thing you start changing is your philosophy, you start changing your mind. You start

changing how you think. You start picking up new ideas and information, gather new knowledge, make better decisions about what's valuable, and I'm telling you if you do that, your whole life will change. Your health will change, your relationship with your family will change, your ability to cope with challenges and problems will change, income, promotions, all of it will change. If you won't change it isn't gonna change."

I have experienced many times in my life where people will talk to me as if they are wanting the best for me. At the same time, they are giving me advice and suggesting that I take some action or follow some path that is completely against what I am trying to accomplish in that moment. It's even more powerful when these types of messages come from a friend or family member. The influence of friends, family members, and others may be very strong at times and many people are likely to give up on their dreams and desires when faced with challenges like this. The idea is to just keep moving forward and keep our vision alive, especially if we are the only ones who can see it. The longer we can hold onto our vision, the closer we get to its manifestation. Once it manifests into reality, people will believe it, and you can usually expect people to ask forgiveness for ever doubting you.

> *"Tell the young high school kids keep dreamin' because they sure do come true" - Drake*

Patience is also imperative if we desire to have peace of mind while on the way toward our creation. Growth takes time and understanding that can help us be more patient in our own growth process. A gardener cannot force a plant to grow. Attempting to force growth only creates resistance. The best way to support growth is to let it happen naturally. When we are impatient, we are giving off a vibration of trying to force growth or change, which will only slow down the process and take us away from our desires. For example, a person who's in a hurry goes to a place like a bank, restaurant, or grocery store, or let's say they call their cell phone company. This person is obviously trying to accomplish something, but they are also impatient and mention several times throughout the interaction that they are in a hurry. Every time this person mentions their rushed state, they stop the conversation from happening and derail the whole process because of impatience. The interaction takes significantly longer compared to someone who is patient and cooperative. Time will bring us closer to our desires no matter what, so the choice to be impatient or get upset with the process is only going to hurt us in the long run.

Creation is not a race, nor is it a competition. There really is no competition unless we make it for ourselves. With the whole world growing and changing, it does not benefit us to focus on others' rates of change or results. Of course we can benefit by observing and learning from others who are in the same field as us, but if we attempt to compete with others, we can easily create stress and stray from our desires. When it comes to creation, it's also important to realize that there is no finish line. Creation is always happening and there is ongoing room to grow, improve, change, learn, and explore. As mentioned earlier, if we decide that we are done creating, we begin a downward spiral and lose our purpose on this earth.

09: MASTER CREATOR/
CONCLUSION

The **power is in your hands**, and it always has been

As we begin to understand more about ourselves and the universe, and start practicing these teachings in our own lives while becoming ever more awake, we will inevitably become one of two types of people. One is awake and aware of the laws of the universe and personally understands their own way of creating with the universe. This person will go on to create amazing things, live an incredible life, and change and inspire many people with their personality and lifestyle. This person mainly keeps their tips and tricks to themselves, mainly because they are so caught up in enjoying their own life and don't feel a need or desire to focus much time and energy on teaching others – and there's nothing wrong with that.

The other type of person is one who is awake and aware of the universe and creation, but this person goes out of their way to teach and help other people learn and understand the workings of humans within the universe. This is not an easy job and takes much time to think and practice working with other people in different situations. It is a completely separate skill from all of those that come with being awake. This skill can be known as leadership. These are the people who start the trends. These are the people who are likely to be followed. If we want people to follow us, we must first be worth following. This means understanding the truth on a personal level, working toward mastering creation, learning about leadership, and improving communication and people skills along the way.

We can not give something we do not have. So in order to give this gift to others and share the abundance, we must first acquire our own wealth of knowledge and skill. It is easy to go around and tell people about these truths, but if we want people to really listen to us, we have to make changes in our own lives because in most cases, words don't teach. Ever heard that saying "Monkey see, monkey do"? This is the same with humans – we are more likely to do what we see other people doing, rather than to do what we hear other people talking about. A good example is a parent who smokes cigarettes and tells their child not to smoke. These are the parents who say "do as I say, not as I do" which is not a very good lesson to teach. Nine times out of ten, the child will pay more attention to the actions rather than the words. If we practice what we preach, people are much more likely to follow in our footsteps and are less likely to resent us.

Whichever person we decide to become, there will be different levels of awakening and many moments of realization and overcoming obstacles. We all have the strength and willpower within us to wake up and live up to our full potential. We are our own worst enemy and the only thing stopping us from becoming the person we want to become is ourselves. If we truly dive into any "reasoning" or excuses for changes not being made or goals not being reached, we will find that there really is nothing in our way. The good news is, it's up to you. The bad news is, it's up to you. You, and only you, can break the mental blocks that separate you from your goals.

When you change the way you look at things, the things you look at change. Beauty is in the eyes of the beholder. These are common maxims and when you understand what is being said, it instantly creates a moment of awakening. When we remember the fact that we shape our own perspective and reality, we really can choose how we see things at any moment. This just shows that our ideas and our reality are just illusions. The universe is designed to create illusions, to trick you, and catch you off guard by throwing different obstacles and perspectives at you. Once you can fully awaken to the truth that we create our own reality, we begin to access one of the most powerful vibrations to the universe. A vibration saying I am ready. When we send the "I am ready" vibration (Abraham Hicks calls it "the receiving mode"), we begin to move closer to all of the abundance that has been stored up from all our past desires and wishes. The longer we can stay in the receiving mode, the more abundance we will attract. And trust me, you want to attract abundance! There is nothing better than getting what you ask for. Even though sometimes we may not like it, we can still be grateful that we did in fact get what we asked for. Of course we may not stay in that grateful vibration forever because for pleasure to exist, there must also be a pain to compare it to. Practicing all of these thoughts daily can grant us permission to some of the most amazing experiences that life has to offer.

Every realization of changing perspective is a moment of awakening and an increase in knowledge and wisdom. Every awakening we have brings us closer to the desires we set in place for ourselves. We are either awakening in a direction for or against our goals and desires. The more goals you have and the more you focus on them, the more they become closer to being a reality. The moment you stop focusing on your goals and desires, you also stop heading toward your desires. This isn't necessarily a bad thing. For example, if I decide to take a vacation and choose to have a few days of fun and relaxation without thinking about any kind of work, it isn't necessarily a bad thing. That momentum will still be there when I get back. If you have concrete goals and a daily routine in place, you can just hop right back into that stream of energy and just let it carry you along like when a river carries along a piece of wood.

If you can change what's inside, you can begin to change what's outside. If you change your perspective, your environment will change. Change is necessary. Things must change. Nothing lasts forever. When we accept change rather than rejecting it, we begin to flow with nature and evolve into the purest version of ourselves. Changing means altering our perspective, vibration, and reaction in relationship with the environment. Of course the environment will change regardless of what you are perceiving. Whatever kind of energy you're giving off, the environment will still change and if we want the environment to change more in our favor, we first have to change our mind. Every event and every moment in life is a continual cycle and recycling of energy. Energy is always flowing through us, whether we are conscious of it or not. When we're asleep, our heart keeps beating, our lungs keep breathing, and our mind stays active in different vibrational states.

Knowing these lessons is like being handed the mask and the powers of a superhero, but like Stan Lee said, "With great power comes great responsibility." The power is in your hands now. What you choose to do with it is completely up to you. Be wise and be careful because what has been given can be taken away. To keep the power of the universe on our side, we can appreciate the fact that we have it, focus on it, and practice it regularly. As long as what we are creating is based on truth and justice, we can expect our life to be amazing. If anything is created with lies and deception as a foundation, it will surely fail and cease to exist. Time reveals everything and all of the lessons in this book have stood the test of time. These lessons are possibly the most important lessons a human being could learn and now they are in your hands.

Some people will stay trapped in these lies and illusions of the past, or the lies and illusions of conformity, and that's their choice, even if they don't realize it. Awakening to our true human potential is like being a magician and knowing the tricks that fool the audience. Once we transcend the classic illusions of life and realize that we are co-creating our reality with the universe, we gain the upper hand in almost every situation. Not to mention, we earn the opportunity to help other people escape the same illusions that used to hold us back, which is absolutely priceless.

Anything that has been given to us can be taken away. Everything that we have on this earth is a gift that was given to us and if we choose to neglect the gifts we have, we will surely lose them. Our mind is a gift, our body is a gift, this earth is a gift, love, peace, and happiness are gifts, and all of these things have been given to us for free. Many people have the tendency to take these gifts for granted and put a value on material things, when in reality, the most valuable things are those things that were given to us for free. These gifts are priceless and when we realize it, we can start respecting them and the more we respect and appreciate them, the more benefits we will reap from them.

Along this path of personal development, there are many great things to look forward to and there are also many things to approach with caution. Greed is one thing that can completely take over a person if they allow it. When many people think about what they want in this day and age, there's a good chance that something on that list of wants or goals cannot be obtained without money. Maybe your goal is simply to have lots of money, but that isn't the only thing we can be greedy about. According to Google, greed is "an intense and selfish desire for something, especially wealth, power, or food." So this is where we need to watch ourselves. We can avoid greed and selfishness by giving. The things we "own" here on this earth are not really ours to keep; we are simply borrowing them. When we die, we cannot take our possessions with us. By keeping this in mind and understanding this key concept, we can give willingly and when we do give, we can witness the extraordinary benefits that come from it.

In my own words, I like to call greed the disease of "more." Once we start realizing that we can have anything we want, it's easy to get into a state of mind where we just want more. More pleasure, more food, more money, more fame. This is one thing that's tough to stop once it gets going, but appreciation is the key here. No matter where you want to be or what you want to create in your life, there must be a balance of appreciating what we have, and appreciating what we have coming to us in the future. Without this balance, we will flip and we can easily suffer. Life is all about balance and we should always try to keep that in mind.

Always remember, we came into this world with nothing, and we are going out the same way. Live life to the fullest and enjoy each moment while it lasts because nothing lasts forever. You can't have life without death. You can't have pain without pleasure. So be ready for anything that comes your way and know that you are a powerful creator, and know that the universe is on your side no matter what. It's never too late to make things right.

Last but not least, most people probably are looking for a quick reference to the steps of creation so here it is. How do we manifest something that we desire?

- Figure out what you want. Ask yourself "what do I desire?". Visualize your desire already being manifested and FEEL the emotions you would feel as if it's already done. *Make sure you do not move into the next steps until this one is completed. If you can't visualize your goal and feel the emotions of it being achieved, you will not have the energy to follow through with the plan when it's time. Once you have decided that your goal truly is something you wish to achieve, Write down goal with a timeframe

- Make a plan/ search for a plan for its achievement. Plan carefully and be patient if you cannot come up with a plan right away. Take your time, do your research and figure out what steps you can start taking. Check the fruit on the tree and be sure you are tuned into a reliable source of information during this process.

- Follow through with the plan, taking daily action and trusting that you will achieve your desire in time. Have patience and be persistent with your actions. Make it a point to move forward or accomplish 1% each day to keep the momentum going. It only takes a few tiny disciplines to turn into one big success. While working and waiting for your desires to come into your life, appreciate where you are, enjoy life, and don't overwork yourself. Make the necessary changes sooner rather than later. Find ways to improve what you're doing constantly and do regular checkups on goals. Celebrate small successes to keep yourself motivated. Trust yourself and trust the universe with the plan and know that any improvisation along the way is usually for the greater good. Take risks and take action when action is required. Sometimes you will need to take a leap of faith to get from where you are to where you want to be. If you never take that leap of faith, you will stay where you are. Be ready for the challenges and failures, and embrace them with all of your heart, knowing that what doesn't kill you can only make you stronger. Mind your words and mind your thoughts throughout this process and avoid the classic traps of greed, selfishness, and wanting more.

- Watch and be ready for your creations to come to life. Then, do it all again for the rest of your life, and never stop growing.

The intended purpose of this book is to serve as a stepping stone in the direction of enlightenment for those seeking it, and to provide value to as many people as humanly possible. I encourage you to share the message of this book with the ones you love. The rewards from making a positive impact on someone's life are priceless and could impact generations to come. Do what's right.

G eazy - "Now imagine it, put the hours in and stay passionate Wasn't blowing money, I was stacking it Figured what the F*** I want to do in life and practiced itPay attention none of this is happening by accident Listen, I don't slack a bitGame plan solid, no cracks in itSaid I want a billion now, nothing less is adequate"

J Cole - "This is my canvas, Ima paint it how I want it baby"

Gandhi - "Be the change you want to see in the world"

A$AP Rocky - "They say wealth is in the mind, not the pocket, I learned that from a very wise man"

Quin XCII - "And I'm hoping that they figure out, it's all about the scenery along the route, no fears and no problems"

Kendrick Lamar - "I am a sinner who's probably gonna sin again, lord forgive me for things I don't understand, sometimes I need to be alone, B**** don't kill my vibe"

Bryson Tiller - "For years and years we waited on this, living in a place folks didn't know exist, surprise motherF***er, we up in this n****s, I said I'm back and I'm so much better I'm so much better, and I won't stop, I can't stop, not now, not never"

Post Malone - "I dreamed it all ever since I was young, they said I would be nothing, now they always say congratulations"

Meek Mill - "What's free? Free is when nobody else can tell us what to be.. Through all the fame you know I stay true, Pray my n****s stay free, made a few mistakes but this ain't where I wanna be"

Kid Cudi - "Ima do just what I want, looking ahead, no turning back, If I fall, if

I die, know I lived it to the fullest, if I fall, if I die, know I lived and missed some bullets"

Lil Yachty - "Everything in life could always be better, don't settle for less 'cause then you miss out on more, Everything in life won't always be pleasure, you work for the treasure just to live even more"

Sara Bareilles - "I know the world turns around, I know the lights are gonna go out, but until they do, I've got nothing to lose"

Lana Del Rey and The Weeknd - "We're the masters of our own fate We're the captains of our own souls There's no need for us to hesitate"

Lana Del Rey - "Sometimes I feel like I've got a war in my mind, I wanna get off but I keep riding the ride. I never really noticed that I had to decide to play someone's game, or live my own life and now I do. I wanna move out of the black and into the blue."

Ed Sheeran - "Love could change the world in a moment, but what do I know"

CPSIA information can be obtained
at www.ICGtesting.com
Printed in the USA
LVHW040727220620
658672LV00004B/977